I0018504

AI and the Future of Work

What Every Professional Needs to Know

THOMPSON CARTER

Table of Content

TABLE OF CONTENTS

INTRODUCTION

Preparing for the Future of Work in an AI-Driven World

In recent years, **Artificial Intelligence (AI)** has made significant strides, moving from being a futuristic concept to a powerful force shaping the way we work, live, and interact with the world. As AI technologies—ranging from machine learning algorithms to robotic process automation—continue to evolve, their impact on the **workforce** becomes ever more profound. Today, AI is transforming industries, automating routine tasks, creating new opportunities, and even redefining the roles of professionals across sectors.

As we stand on the brink of an AI-driven workforce, it is clear that the future of work will look radically different from what we know today. This transformation brings with it immense potential but also significant challenges. The rise of AI promises to make businesses more efficient, boost productivity, and open new avenues for growth. However, it also raises important questions about **job displacement**, **skills gaps**, **inequality**, and the ethical implications of AI's presence in the workplace.

This book, *Preparing for the Future: How to Adapt to AI in the Workplace*, is designed to help you navigate this transition. Whether you are a **professional** seeking to future-proof your career, a **business leader** looking to implement AI responsibly, or an **enthusiast** interested in understanding how AI is reshaping the workforce, this book provides the **practical insights**, **strategies**, and **real-world examples** you need to thrive in an AI-driven world.

Why This Book Matters

AI is no longer just the domain of researchers and engineers—it is increasingly accessible to professionals in all fields. From **marketing** and **finance** to **education** and **healthcare**, AI is infiltrating every aspect of the workforce. As AI systems become more integrated into work processes, employees must adapt to new tools and ways of working. The future of work will not simply involve using AI tools but will require a fundamental shift in how we approach learning, problem-solving, creativity, and collaboration.

While AI has the potential to create exciting new roles, it also threatens to displace jobs, particularly in sectors where automation can replace repetitive or manual tasks. In order to **stay competitive** and relevant, professionals must embrace **continuous learning**, **upskilling**, and **reskilling**. The ability to **adapt** to new technologies, understand their implications, and use them to your advantage will be the defining skill of tomorrow's workforce.

However, the impact of AI is not limited to job creation and displacement alone. It also introduces profound ethical, social, and policy questions. Issues such as **AI**

bias, **privacy concerns**, and the **future of human work** need to be addressed with care and foresight. Governments, businesses, and individuals must work together to ensure that AI is deployed in a responsible manner, one that promotes fairness, transparency, and social good.

What You Will Learn

This book will guide you through the steps you need to take to **prepare** for the future of work, where AI will play an ever-larger role. The chapters are designed to equip you with the tools to understand **AI's impact** on your industry, **adapt to new technologies**, and **thrive** in an AI-driven world. Here's what you can expect to learn:

- **Practical strategies** for professionals to **thrive** in an AI-driven workforce, including how to use AI as a tool for augmentation and how to develop the **right skills** for the future.
- The **importance of continuous learning** and **adaptability**, and how to cultivate a **growth mindset** to remain competitive as AI evolves.
- Real-world examples of industries and companies that have successfully **future-proofed their workforce** by embracing AI, such as the use of AI in **healthcare, disaster relief, human resources**, and more.
- **Ethical challenges** of AI in the workplace, including how to address **job displacement, bias, fairness**, and **privacy** concerns.

- How **governments** and **organizations** are creating policies and regulations to ensure AI adoption is responsible, transparent, and beneficial for society.

Why AI is the Future of Work

The role of AI in the workforce is not just about automation or reducing human labor; it's about **empowering people** to do their best work. AI will free individuals from monotonous tasks and give them the ability to focus on **more meaningful, complex, and creative work**. However, this shift requires **adaptability**, as workers will need to master new tools and technologies to unlock the potential of AI.

AI will also create new job opportunities that don't exist yet, particularly in fields like **data science**, **AI engineering**, and **robotics**. However, this shift comes with the challenge of preparing for these roles and ensuring that **workers** from all sectors have access to the **skills** and **training** necessary to fill these new positions.

By understanding **AI's impact on the workforce** and proactively preparing for the future, you can position yourself to thrive, rather than be left behind. In this book, we will provide actionable insights that can help you make the transition into the AI-driven workforce, including how to leverage your existing skills and gain new ones that will make you an invaluable asset in tomorrow's job market.

The Road Ahead

This book is structured to give you a comprehensive understanding of AI's impact on the workforce and offer practical advice on how to **adapt** and **succeed**. Each chapter focuses on a different aspect of AI in the workplace, from **understanding AI** and its potential applications, to **adapting your career** and ensuring that your skills remain relevant in an ever-changing job market.

As we look ahead to the future of work, we can't predict exactly how AI will evolve or how it will affect every industry. But by reading this book, you'll be better prepared to navigate this uncertain future with confidence, knowing that you are equipped with the knowledge and strategies needed to **embrace AI** and use it to **enhance your career**.

Whether you're just beginning your career, considering a shift to a more AI-driven role, or looking to integrate AI into your existing profession, this book will provide you with the tools to **adapt**, **learn**, and **thrive**. The future of work is coming, and with the right mindset and skills, you can not only survive in this new world but also **excel** in it.

CHAPTER 1

Introduction to AI and Its Impact on Work

Defining AI and Its Core Concepts

Artificial Intelligence (AI) refers to the simulation of human intelligence in machines that are programmed to think and act like humans. AI systems can analyze data, recognize patterns, make decisions, and even learn from experiences, mimicking cognitive functions typically associated with human minds. The field of AI encompasses various subfields, each contributing to different types of intelligent behavior.

1. **Machine Learning (ML)**: A subset of AI focused on developing algorithms that allow machines to learn from and make predictions based on data. ML systems improve their performance over time without being explicitly programmed.
    - o **Example**: A recommendation system on an e-commerce website that suggests products based on previous purchases or browsing behavior.
2. **Natural Language Processing (NLP)**: The branch of AI that helps machines understand, interpret, and respond to human language, both written and spoken.
    - o **Example**: Virtual assistants like Siri or Alexa, which process voice commands to

perform tasks like setting reminders or playing music.

3. **Computer Vision**: A field of AI that enables computers to interpret and make decisions based on visual data, such as images and videos.
   - **Example**: Facial recognition systems used for security or identifying customers in retail environments.

4. **Robotics**: The integration of AI with robots to allow them to perform tasks autonomously, often in real-time.
   - **Example**: Industrial robots in manufacturing plants that assemble products with minimal human intervention.

The History of AI in the Workplace

AI's journey in the workplace can be traced back to the mid-20th century, when the first theoretical ideas about machine intelligence began to take shape.

1. **Early Beginnings (1950s-1960s)**:
   - The concept of AI was introduced in the 1950s, with the pioneering work of **Alan Turing** and the development of the **Turing Test**, which proposed a way of measuring a machine's ability to exhibit intelligent behavior. During this time, researchers focused on symbolic AI, developing algorithms to simulate reasoning and problem-solving tasks.

- o Early AI research was heavily theoretical, with little practical application in the workplace.
2. **First AI Applications (1970s-1980s)**:
   - o In the 1970s, AI research began to focus on specific domains, such as **expert systems**—computer programs designed to mimic human expertise in fields like medicine and finance. These systems were used for tasks like medical diagnosis or tax preparation.
   - o **Real-world Example**: **MYCIN**, an expert system developed in the 1970s, was able to diagnose bacterial infections based on input symptoms, demonstrating the early potential of AI in healthcare.
3. **AI and Automation (1990s-2000s)**:
   - o By the 1990s, AI started to make its way into industries like **manufacturing** and **finance**, where automation systems were used to streamline production and reduce costs. In finance, AI-powered algorithms began to assist with tasks like risk management and fraud detection.
   - o **Example**: **Automated teller machines (ATMs)** in banking, which use AI to process transactions and detect fraud patterns in real-time.
4. **AI's Expansion in the 2010s and Beyond**:
   - o The 2010s marked a significant leap in AI development, driven by advancements in **deep learning** and the availability of large datasets. This era saw AI systems

becoming more practical and widely adopted across industries.

- o Companies like **Amazon**, **Google**, and **IBM** developed AI-powered tools that could analyze big data, automate customer service, and optimize supply chains. AI began to be used in fields such as **healthcare**, **customer service**, and **marketing** on a large scale.

How AI is Changing Industries and Professions

AI is rapidly reshaping industries and professions by automating tasks, enhancing productivity, and enabling new ways of working. Here are several ways AI is transforming the workplace:

1. **Automation of Repetitive Tasks**:
   - o AI-powered automation tools are being deployed to handle mundane, repetitive tasks across various industries, freeing up human workers to focus on more complex and creative responsibilities. This is particularly common in sectors like **manufacturing**, **customer service**, and **finance**.
   - o **Example**: In **accounting**, AI software can automatically process invoices, reconcile financial records, and prepare tax filings, tasks that traditionally required significant human involvement.
2. **Enhanced Decision-Making**:

- o AI allows businesses to make more informed and data-driven decisions by analyzing vast amounts of data in real-time and identifying patterns that humans may overlook. This is especially valuable in industries such as **marketing**, **healthcare**, and **finance**, where data is abundant, and decisions need to be quick and accurate.
- o **Example**: **AI-powered financial advisors** that analyze market trends and provide investment advice tailored to an individual's risk profile and goals.

3. **Personalized Experiences**:
   - o AI is enhancing customer experiences by providing personalized recommendations, services, and content. Companies can use AI to tailor their offerings based on individual preferences, browsing history, and behavior.
   - o **Example**: In **retail**, companies like **Amazon** and **Netflix** use AI to personalize product and content recommendations, boosting sales and engagement.

4. **Augmenting Human Capabilities**:
   - o Rather than replacing human workers, AI is often used to augment their abilities. AI tools can assist workers by offering real-time insights, providing recommendations, or helping with complex tasks. For example, in **healthcare**, AI can assist doctors in

diagnosing diseases, interpreting medical images, and recommending treatment plans.

- o **Example**: **AI-driven diagnostic tools** like **IBM Watson Health** can analyze medical data to assist doctors in diagnosing conditions more accurately and efficiently.

5. **Creating New Job Roles**:
   - o While AI may automate some tasks, it is also creating new job roles and professions. There is increasing demand for **AI specialists**, **data scientists**, and professionals who can develop, implement, and manage AI systems.
   - o **Example**: The rise of **data science** as a profession is directly tied to the increasing reliance on AI and big data analytics across industries.

6. **Changing the Nature of Work**:
   - o AI is altering how professionals approach their work by enabling more remote collaboration, automating time-consuming tasks, and enhancing flexibility. It is shifting the focus from repetitive, manual work to higher-level problem-solving, creative thinking, and innovation.
   - o **Example**: In **project management**, AI tools help streamline scheduling, task assignments, and resource management, allowing managers to focus more on

strategic decision-making and team dynamics.

Real-World Example: AI in Customer Service

AI is revolutionizing customer service by enabling businesses to offer quicker, more personalized, and efficient support. AI-powered tools like **chatbots** and **virtual assistants** are increasingly being used to handle routine customer queries, complaints, and support tickets, allowing human agents to focus on more complex issues.

1. **Chatbots**:
    o AI-driven chatbots can interact with customers in real time, answering their questions, resolving common issues, and guiding them through basic processes. These bots use natural language processing (NLP) to understand customer inquiries and provide relevant responses.
    o **Example: H&M's chatbot**, powered by AI, helps customers find the right clothing sizes, track orders, and even suggest outfits, all through conversational interactions.

2. **Virtual Assistants**:
    o Virtual assistants like **Siri**, **Alexa**, and **Google Assistant** are also making their way into customer service, helping users navigate websites, check account balances, and schedule appointments. These assistants use AI to understand

voice commands and deliver personalized responses.

  - o **Example**: **Sephora's Virtual Artist** is an AI-powered assistant that helps customers try on makeup virtually, suggest products, and provide beauty tips based on their preferences.

3. **AI-Powered Support Ticketing Systems**:

  - o AI systems are also used to automate the management of customer support tickets. AI can categorize and prioritize tickets, assign them to the appropriate agents, and even resolve simple issues without human intervention.

  - o **Example**: **Zendesk's AI-powered platform** helps companies like **Airbnb** and **Shopify** automatically route support tickets to the right department, track customer inquiries, and ensure efficient resolution.

4. **Sentiment Analysis**:

  - o AI can also analyze customer feedback through **sentiment analysis**, identifying whether customers are satisfied, frustrated, or indifferent based on the language they use. This allows businesses to respond proactively to customer concerns and improve overall service quality.

  - o **Example**: **LivePerson**, an AI-powered messaging platform, uses sentiment analysis to help companies understand customer emotions and tailor their responses accordingly, improving satisfaction rates.

Summary

In this chapter, we explored the definition of AI and its core concepts, such as **machine learning, natural language processing**, and **computer vision**, all of which are shaping the future of work. We also traced the history of AI's application in the workplace, from early expert systems to the AI-driven revolution in industries today. AI's impact on industries and professions is profound, with automation, enhanced decision-making, and the creation of new job roles at the forefront of this transformation. Lastly, we highlighted a **real-world example** of AI in **customer service**, where AI tools like chatbots, virtual assistants, and support ticketing systems are revolutionizing how businesses interact with their customers.

AI is not just a passing trend—it is a profound shift that is redefining what work means in the 21st century. As AI continues to evolve, it's essential for professionals to understand its capabilities, implications, and potential. The future of work is undeniably intertwined with AI, and those who can adapt will thrive in this new era of technology-driven transformation.

CHAPTER 2

The Rise of Automation: What's Changing?

What Automation Means in the Context of Work

Automation in the context of work refers to the use of technology—particularly **AI**, **robotics**, and **machine learning**—to perform tasks traditionally carried out by humans. These tasks can range from repetitive manual labor to complex data analysis, and automation is increasingly being applied across a wide array of industries to improve efficiency, reduce costs, and eliminate human error.

1. **Basic Definition**:
    o At its core, automation involves using machines or software to carry out tasks with minimal human intervention. In a workplace setting, this often means replacing manual, repetitive, or routine tasks with automated systems that can perform them more efficiently and accurately.
    o **Example**: In a **call center**, automated phone systems (or **IVR systems**) answer customer inquiries, route calls, and even resolve basic problems, freeing up human agents to address more complex customer needs.
2. **Levels of Automation**:

- o Automation can range from simple **task automation**, where specific actions are performed automatically, to more **complex process automation**, where entire workflows and decision-making processes are handled by machines.
- o **Example**: **Task automation** might involve software that automatically fills out forms, while **process automation** could involve an AI system managing the entire order-to-delivery process in a supply chain.

3. **Automation's Role in Redefining Work**:
   - o Automation is reshaping what it means to "work." In many cases, it's not about eliminating jobs, but transforming them. Humans are increasingly required to oversee automated systems, make complex decisions, and focus on tasks that require creativity, empathy, and complex judgment.
   - o **Example**: In **healthcare**, while AI can automate diagnostic tasks and process medical images, healthcare professionals still play a critical role in making treatment decisions and interacting with patients.

AI's Role in Automating Routine Tasks

AI plays a central role in driving automation in the workplace by applying advanced algorithms to automate routine and time-consuming tasks. AI systems can analyze data, recognize patterns, and make decisions faster and more accurately than humans, making them highly effective at automating tasks that were traditionally labor-intensive.

1. **Repetitive Administrative Tasks**:
   - Many administrative tasks, such as scheduling meetings, processing invoices, or managing emails, are ripe for automation with AI. AI systems can quickly perform these repetitive tasks, freeing up human workers to focus on higher-level, more strategic work.
   - **Example**: In **accounting**, AI-powered software can automatically categorize transactions, generate financial reports, and even flag discrepancies, reducing the amount of manual labor involved in financial analysis.

2. **Data-Driven Decision Making**:
   - AI is also increasingly used to automate data-driven decision-making. By analyzing vast amounts of data, AI systems can generate insights, predict trends, and make recommendations with little human intervention.
   - **Example**: In **marketing**, AI can automate the creation of targeted ads and campaigns based on customer data, ensuring that the right message is delivered to the right audience at the right time.

3. **Customer Service Automation**:

- o In customer service, AI-driven chatbots and virtual assistants can automate many routine tasks, such as answering frequently asked questions, resolving simple issues, and guiding customers through troubleshooting steps. This improves response times and provides customers with quicker resolutions to common problems.
- o **Example**: **Chatbots** on websites or through messaging apps can help customers check order statuses, track deliveries, or resolve basic service inquiries without requiring human intervention.

4. **AI in Manufacturing**:
- o AI-powered robots in manufacturing environments can automate repetitive tasks such as assembling parts, sorting materials, or packaging products. These robots can perform tasks at a much faster pace and with higher precision than humans, contributing to greater efficiency on the production line.
- o **Example**: In **automotive manufacturing**, robots are used to assemble car parts, weld components, and install parts like windows or engines, all of which were previously labor-intensive tasks.

Examples of Industries Benefiting from Automation

Automation is having a profound impact across many industries, helping businesses save costs, increase productivity, and enhance accuracy. Below are some key industries where automation, powered by AI and robotics, is creating significant changes.

1. **Manufacturing**:
   o Automation has long been a staple in manufacturing, with robots and AI systems taking on repetitive, dangerous, or precision-critical tasks. From car assembly lines to electronics manufacturing, automation is increasing production rates while minimizing human error.
   o **Example**: **Tesla's Gigafactory** utilizes AI-powered robots for the production of electric vehicles, automating tasks such as painting, welding, and final assembly.
2. **Retail**:
   o In retail, automation is used for inventory management, order fulfillment, and personalized customer experiences. AI algorithms help businesses predict customer demand, manage stock levels, and automate the recommendation of products to consumers.
   o **Example**: **Amazon** uses AI-powered robots to retrieve items in its warehouses and package them for delivery, making

the order fulfillment process faster and more efficient.

3. **Finance**:
    o The financial industry is leveraging automation to improve fraud detection, enhance risk management, and speed up financial transactions. AI is also automating tasks such as compliance checks, portfolio management, and customer service.
    o **Example**: **Robo-advisors**, like those offered by **Wealthfront** or **Betterment**, use AI to automate investment management, providing personalized financial advice based on algorithms rather than human advisors.

4. **Healthcare**:
    o AI and automation are making significant strides in healthcare, automating tasks such as **medical imaging analysis**, **patient monitoring**, and **drug discovery**. These technologies not only save time but also help improve diagnostic accuracy and treatment outcomes.
    o **Example**: **IBM Watson Health** uses AI to analyze medical records and assist doctors in diagnosing diseases, as well as suggesting treatment plans based on large datasets of medical knowledge.

5. **Transportation and Logistics**:
    o In transportation, automation is improving both passenger experiences and supply chain operations. AI-powered

systems are used for route optimization, predictive maintenance, and self-driving vehicles.

- o **Example**: **Self-driving trucks**, being tested by companies like **Waymo** and **Tesla**, are set to revolutionize logistics by automating long-haul freight transport, reducing reliance on human drivers.

6. **Customer Service**:
   - o Customer service industries are leveraging automation to streamline support processes. AI-powered systems like chatbots, virtual assistants, and automated phone systems can handle routine inquiries, leaving human agents to focus on complex issues.
   - o **Example**: **Banking institutions** are using AI to automate customer service functions like balance inquiries, transaction processing, and fraud detection, improving service response times and customer satisfaction.

Real-World Example: Robotics in Manufacturing

One of the most prominent and widespread applications of automation is in **manufacturing**, where **robotics** has significantly changed how products are made. Robots, often powered by AI, are used to perform tasks that would otherwise be time-consuming, dangerous, or repetitive for human workers.

1. **Automotive Manufacturing**:

- In the automotive industry, robots have been used for decades to automate tasks like welding, painting, and assembling car parts. These robots not only increase the speed and accuracy of production but also enhance worker safety by taking on dangerous tasks, such as handling toxic chemicals or working in hazardous environments.
- **Example**: **General Motors (GM)** and **Ford** use robotic arms and AI-driven systems to handle tasks such as body welding, door assembly, and painting, making the process faster and reducing the likelihood of errors.

2. **Electronics Manufacturing**:
   - Robotics is also widely used in the electronics manufacturing sector. Robots assemble small, delicate components with precision, ensuring that parts like circuit boards, semiconductors, and smartphones are built to exact specifications. AI systems optimize the entire assembly line process, ensuring high throughput and minimal waste.
   - **Example**: **Foxconn**, a major electronics manufacturer, uses thousands of robots in its production lines for companies like **Apple** to assemble mobile devices. These robots are programmed to perform tasks like screwing in small parts, attaching screens, and testing the functionality of each device.

3. **Pharmaceutical Manufacturing**:
   - In pharmaceutical manufacturing, robots help automate the mixing, bottling, and labeling of medications. This automation ensures consistent quality and compliance with regulatory standards, such as **Good Manufacturing Practices (GMP)**.
   - **Example**: **Robotic arms** in pharmaceutical plants are used to handle drugs in high-speed environments, improving the consistency and reliability of the manufacturing process.
4. **Food and Beverage Industry**:
   - The food and beverage industry also benefits from robotics, with machines handling everything from packaging and labeling to processing and sorting ingredients. AI ensures the efficiency of production lines and maintains quality control by monitoring the process in real-time.
   - **Example**: In **chicken processing plants**, robots automate the tasks of cutting and sorting, which are repetitive and labor-intensive, reducing human labor and improving efficiency.

Summary

In this chapter, we explored the rise of **automation** and its profound impact on the workplace. We defined automation in the context of work and discussed how **AI** is driving the automation of routine tasks, allowing businesses to improve efficiency, reduce costs, and enhance productivity. Industries such as **manufacturing**, **retail**, **finance**, and **healthcare** are all benefiting from automation, with AI systems streamlining processes and providing real-time insights.

We also provided a **real-world example** of **robotics in manufacturing**, highlighting how robots are transforming production lines in industries like **automotive**, **electronics**, and **food production**. As automation continues to advance, its impact on the workforce will only grow, reshaping the nature of work and creating new opportunities for innovation and efficiency.

As professionals adapt to this new landscape, understanding how automation works and how to leverage it in their respective fields will be essential for staying competitive and effective in an increasingly AI-driven world.

CHAPTER 3

Understanding Machine Learning and Its Role in Work

The Basics of Machine Learning (ML)

Machine Learning (ML) is a subset of artificial intelligence (AI) that enables systems to automatically learn and improve from experience without being explicitly programmed. It is based on the idea that systems can identify patterns in data, make predictions, and adapt to new situations by leveraging these patterns. ML algorithms use large amounts of data to train a model, which can then be used to make decisions or predictions.

1. **Key Concepts in Machine Learning**:
    o **Data**: The foundation of ML, as the algorithm learns from data to make predictions or decisions. The more data a system is trained on, the more accurate its predictions are likely to be.
    o **Algorithms**: Mathematical models that ML systems use to analyze data and identify patterns. Common types include decision trees, neural networks, and regression models.
    o **Training**: The process where an ML model learns from labeled data (supervised learning) or raw data (unsupervised learning) and adjusts its

internal parameters to improve its accuracy.

- o **Prediction**: After training, an ML model can use new, unseen data to predict outcomes, identify trends, or classify information based on the patterns it has learned.

2. **How Machine Learning Works**:

- o Machine learning typically starts with a dataset. The algorithm analyzes this dataset to find correlations, patterns, or features that can be used to make predictions. Depending on the type of learning, it may be provided with labeled data (supervised) or learn to identify hidden structures within the data on its own (unsupervised).
- o Once the model is trained, it is tested with new data, and adjustments are made to improve its performance.

Supervised vs. Unsupervised Learning

Machine learning is generally divided into two main categories: **supervised learning** and **unsupervised learning**. Each approach has distinct applications, advantages, and limitations, and is used in different work environments based on the nature of the data and the desired outcome.

1. **Supervised Learning**:

- o **Definition**: In supervised learning, the machine is trained using labeled data.

Each data point is associated with a correct label or outcome, and the model learns to map input data to the corresponding labels. The goal is for the model to make predictions based on new, unseen data using the patterns it has learned from the labeled training data.

- o **How it Works**: The model receives both the input and the corresponding output during the training phase, and the algorithm continuously adjusts itself to minimize the error in its predictions.
- o **Applications**: Supervised learning is commonly used in tasks where the desired output is known, such as **classification** (e.g., spam detection, image classification) or **regression** (e.g., predicting house prices or stock market trends).
- o **Real-world Example**: A supervised learning model could be used to **predict employee performance** in a company, based on labeled historical data about employee performance metrics.

2. **Unsupervised Learning**:
- o **Definition**: In unsupervised learning, the model is provided with data that is not labeled, meaning there is no explicit output for the algorithm to learn from. The goal here is for the model to identify patterns, relationships, or clusters in the data on its own.

- o **How it Works**: Unsupervised learning algorithms try to organize data into groups or structures that make sense, based on the features of the data.
- o **Applications**: Unsupervised learning is commonly used for **clustering** (e.g., grouping customers by purchasing behavior) or **dimensionality reduction** (e.g., reducing the complexity of data while retaining important features).
- o **Real-world Example**: Unsupervised learning is often used in **customer segmentation** in marketing, where the system identifies distinct groups of customers based on their buying habits, without requiring predefined labels for each customer.

3. **Comparison**:
   - o **Supervised Learning**: Best used when the desired outcome is known and labeled data is available. It's more accurate for making predictions on new data based on historical patterns.
   - o **Unsupervised Learning**: Best used when the desired outcome is not known, and the goal is to discover hidden patterns, relationships, or groupings in the data.

Applications of ML in Work Environments

Machine learning is transforming work environments by automating tasks, improving decision-making, and optimizing processes across industries. From data-driven insights to predictive modeling, ML is increasingly integrated into various workflows, helping organizations make smarter, faster decisions and improving efficiency.

1. **Marketing and Sales**:
   o Machine learning is used to personalize marketing strategies, predict customer preferences, and optimize sales funnels. By analyzing past customer interactions and behaviors, ML algorithms can predict future purchasing patterns and suggest targeted marketing strategies.
   o **Example**: **Netflix** and **Amazon** use ML algorithms to recommend movies, TV shows, and products based on users' browsing history, improving customer engagement and increasing sales.

2. **Healthcare**:
   o ML is making a huge impact in healthcare by improving diagnostics, treatment plans, and patient outcomes. Algorithms can analyze medical data to detect patterns in patient records, predict health risks, and assist in diagnosing conditions such as cancer, heart disease, or diabetes.
   o **Example: IBM Watson Health** uses ML to analyze patient data and recommend treatment options, helping doctors make more informed decisions and improving patient outcomes.

3. **Finance and Banking**:

o In finance, machine learning is used for fraud detection, credit scoring, algorithmic trading, and risk management. ML algorithms can analyze large datasets to spot unusual patterns, predict financial trends, and assess the likelihood of fraud or financial instability.

o **Example**: Banks use ML algorithms to detect fraudulent activity by monitoring transaction patterns and flagging suspicious behavior in real time.

4. **Manufacturing and Supply Chain**:

o Machine learning is used to optimize manufacturing processes, predict equipment failures, and streamline supply chains. By analyzing data from production lines and supply networks, ML algorithms can predict maintenance needs, optimize stock levels, and improve delivery times.

o **Example**: **General Electric (GE)** uses machine learning to predict when turbines and industrial equipment will need maintenance, reducing downtime and improving operational efficiency.

5. **Customer Service**:

o Machine learning plays a major role in automating customer service operations. Chatbots powered by ML are able to handle simple customer inquiries, while more advanced systems can analyze customer sentiment and provide personalized responses based on previous interactions.

- o **Example**: **Zendesk** and **Freshdesk** use ML to automate customer support, from ticket categorization to routing queries to the appropriate human agents, improving response times and customer satisfaction.

6. **Human Resources (HR)**:
    - o ML is increasingly used in HR for tasks like **recruitment,** **employee performance tracking**, and **talent management**. By analyzing resumes, interview feedback, and employee performance data, ML algorithms can help HR professionals identify the best candidates, predict employee success, and identify opportunities for employee development.
    - o **Example**: **HireVue** uses AI-powered video interview analysis, enabling companies to evaluate candidates' responses and predict their suitability for a role.

Real-World Example: ML in HR Recruitment Tools

Machine learning is particularly impactful in **Human Resources (HR)**, where it is used to streamline recruitment, improve decision-making, and enhance employee engagement. One key area where ML is transforming HR is in the **recruitment process**, helping companies identify top talent more efficiently and fairly.

1. **Automated Resume Screening**:
   o ML algorithms can be used to scan resumes and match candidates with job descriptions, automatically ranking applicants based on their qualifications and experience. This saves HR professionals significant time and effort by removing the need to manually review each resume.
   o **Example**: **HireVue** offers an AI-powered recruitment tool that analyzes video interviews to assess candidates' responses, facial expressions, and tone of voice, alongside their written resumes, to determine their suitability for a role.

2. **Predicting Employee Success**:
   o Machine learning models can analyze historical employee performance data to identify the traits, skills, and backgrounds of employees who perform well in specific roles. This helps HR departments make better hiring decisions and reduces the risk of bad hires.
   o **Example**: **Pymetrics** uses AI to assess candidates' cognitive and emotional traits through a series of neuroscience-based games. The tool then compares these traits with those of successful employees within the company to match candidates with roles they are likely to succeed in.

3. **Bias Reduction in Recruitment**:
   o ML can help reduce bias in hiring decisions by ensuring that recruitment

decisions are based on objective data rather than subjective human judgment. By analyzing large datasets, AI can identify unconscious biases in the hiring process and make more equitable recommendations.

- o **Example**: **Unilever** uses AI to remove biases in their recruitment process. They use ML algorithms to analyze video interview responses and resumes, focusing on candidates' skills and experience rather than their gender or background, ensuring a more diverse and fair hiring process.

4. **Employee Engagement and Retention**:
   - o Machine learning can also be used to analyze employee engagement and satisfaction levels, predict potential turnover, and provide insights into how to improve employee retention. By processing feedback surveys, performance reviews, and social media activity, ML algorithms can help HR departments take proactive steps to retain top talent.
   - o **Example**: **IBM Watson Talent** uses machine learning to analyze employee sentiment, job satisfaction, and career progression, allowing HR teams to identify potential flight risks and offer solutions to improve employee retention.

Summary

In this chapter, we covered the basics of **machine learning (ML)** and its significant role in transforming work environments. We discussed the key differences between **supervised** and **unsupervised learning**, each of which plays a pivotal role in various industries. ML is increasingly being applied in **marketing**, **healthcare**, **finance**, **manufacturing**, **customer service**, and **human resources**, automating processes, enhancing decision-making, and optimizing workflows.

A real-world example of ML in **HR recruitment tools** highlighted how AI is being used to streamline recruitment, improve candidate selection, reduce bias, and enhance employee engagement. From automating resume screening to predicting employee success, machine learning is reshaping how HR professionals manage talent and create fairer, more efficient hiring processes.

As machine learning continues to evolve, its impact on work will only grow, offering new ways for professionals to leverage data, enhance productivity, and make better, more informed decisions.

CHAPTER 4

AI and Data: The New Workforce

The Power of Data in Driving AI Decisions

In today's world, data is often referred to as the "new oil," a critical asset for businesses across industries. For AI to function effectively, it relies heavily on data to **train** algorithms, **make decisions**, and **predict outcomes**. The power of AI lies in its ability to process vast amounts of data far faster and more accurately than any human can, uncovering insights, patterns, and correlations that were once impossible to detect.

1. **Data as the Foundation of AI**:
   o AI models, such as machine learning and deep learning, require large datasets to learn and make decisions. The more data these systems can access, the better they become at recognizing patterns and making accurate predictions. This is particularly true in applications such as **image recognition**, **speech recognition**, **recommendation engines**, and **predictive analytics**.
   o **Example**: In **natural language processing (NLP)**, AI algorithms are trained on vast corpora of text to understand language, context, and meaning. For AI systems like **chatbots** or **virtual assistants** to provide useful responses, they must be trained on large

datasets of dialogues to "learn" how humans communicate.

2. **Data-Driven Decisions**:
   - AI systems can make decisions by analyzing data from various sources, such as historical records, real-time data feeds, and sensory inputs. This ability to derive actionable insights from data is at the core of many AI-driven applications in industries ranging from **finance** to **healthcare** to **marketing**.
   - **Example**: In **marketing**, AI systems analyze consumer behavior and purchasing patterns to create personalized ad campaigns, enhancing the customer experience and improving sales.

3. **The Role of Big Data**:
   - The advent of **big data** has significantly expanded AI's capabilities. With access to vast amounts of data—often referred to as "big data"—AI can learn and adapt more quickly, make more informed decisions, and predict outcomes with higher accuracy. This has profound implications for industries that deal with large, complex datasets, such as **healthcare**, **finance**, and **logistics**.
   - **Example**: **Amazon** and **Netflix** use big data to personalize recommendations for their users. They analyze your past purchases, viewing history, and browsing behavior to predict what products or

shows you are most likely to buy or watch next.

How AI Uses Data to Improve Workflows

AI leverages data not just to make decisions, but also to optimize **workflows**, increase **efficiency**, and reduce the potential for human error. By automating data-driven processes, AI frees up human workers from repetitive tasks, enabling them to focus on more strategic and creative activities.

1. **Optimizing Operations**:
    o AI algorithms are used to optimize operations in various industries by analyzing performance data, identifying inefficiencies, and suggesting improvements. This is especially useful in fields such as **supply chain management**, **manufacturing**, and **energy management**, where small improvements can lead to significant cost savings.
    o **Example**: In **logistics**, companies like **UPS** use AI to optimize delivery routes. The system analyzes real-time traffic data, historical delivery patterns, and weather conditions to determine the most efficient routes, saving time and fuel.
2. **Enhancing Productivity**:
    o AI can automate routine tasks, allowing employees to focus on higher-level, value-added work. For instance, in

finance, AI can automate the analysis of financial reports and transactions, freeing up analysts to focus on strategy and advising clients.

- **Example**: **AI-powered chatbots** in customer service can handle thousands of customer inquiries at once, answering basic questions, processing transactions, or even resolving complaints, while human agents handle more complex issues.

3. **Improving Decision-Making**:
   - AI uses data to generate actionable insights that help businesses make better decisions. Whether it's predicting market trends, assessing credit risk, or improving customer satisfaction, AI algorithms analyze data to provide insights that human workers may overlook or take too long to uncover.
   - **Example**: In **healthcare**, AI-powered systems analyze medical records, lab results, and imaging data to help doctors make more accurate diagnoses, recommend treatments, and predict patient outcomes.

4. **Real-Time Data Analysis**:
   - AI can process **real-time data** to make decisions on the fly. This is particularly useful in industries such as **transportation**, **energy**, and **retail**, where decisions need to be made quickly to respond to changing conditions.

- Example: In **retail**, AI systems use real-time data to adjust pricing dynamically based on demand, inventory levels, and competitor prices. This helps stores optimize their pricing strategies and maximize profits.

Ethical Considerations in Data Collection and Usage

While data is crucial for driving AI, its collection and usage raise significant ethical issues, particularly regarding **privacy**, **bias**, **transparency**, and **consent**. As AI systems become more reliant on data to make decisions, it is essential to ensure that the data is collected, managed, and used in ways that respect individuals' rights and promote fairness.

1. **Data Privacy**:
   - As AI systems collect vast amounts of personal data, **privacy concerns** become more pronounced. People must have control over how their data is collected, stored, and shared, and organizations must ensure that they are compliant with **data protection laws**, such as the **General Data Protection Regulation (GDPR)** in the European Union.
   - Example: Social media platforms like **Facebook** and **Google** collect vast amounts of personal data for targeted advertising. However, they have faced scrutiny over how that data is used and

whether users have sufficient control over their information.

2. **Bias in Data**:
   - One of the biggest challenges in AI is addressing **bias** in the data that feeds AI systems. If AI models are trained on biased data, they can reinforce or perpetuate unfair outcomes, leading to **discrimination** in decision-making processes such as hiring, lending, or law enforcement.
   - **Example**: **AI in hiring tools** has been shown to favor certain demographics over others due to biased historical data. For instance, AI recruitment tools trained on historical data from predominantly male workforces might unintentionally discriminate against female applicants.

3. **Transparency and Accountability**:
   - As AI systems become more complex, it becomes harder to understand how decisions are made. This lack of **transparency** can erode trust in AI systems, particularly in high-stakes areas like **criminal justice** or **healthcare**. It's essential that organizations provide clear explanations of how their AI systems work, the data they use, and the potential consequences of their decisions.
   - **Example**: In **predictive policing**, AI systems analyze historical crime data to predict where crimes are likely to occur. However, the lack of transparency in how

these models make decisions can lead to unfair outcomes, particularly in marginalized communities, without clear accountability.

4. **Consent and Control**:
   - AI systems often rely on **consent** from individuals to use their data. It's essential that organizations obtain explicit consent from individuals before collecting and using their data, and that users have the ability to withdraw consent and delete their data.
   - **Example**: **Health apps** that collect personal health data should clearly inform users about what data is being collected, how it will be used, and how long it will be retained, allowing users to control their data.

Real-World Example: Data-Driven Decision-Making in Finance

The finance industry has been one of the early adopters of data-driven decision-making powered by AI. In areas such as **risk management**, **fraud detection**, and **credit scoring**, AI is transforming how financial institutions process data and make decisions.

1. **Risk Assessment**:
   - AI-powered systems can analyze large datasets, such as financial records, market trends, and macroeconomic factors, to assess the risk associated with different

financial assets or investments. These systems can make predictions about the future performance of stocks, bonds, or other financial instruments.

- o **Example**: **Goldman Sachs** and **JP Morgan** use AI models to predict stock prices and analyze potential risks in their investment portfolios. These systems help investment managers make better-informed decisions and optimize portfolio allocations.

2. **Fraud Detection**:
   - o AI systems are also used in fraud detection by analyzing transactional data in real time and identifying suspicious activity. By identifying patterns in data, AI can flag transactions that are unusual or potentially fraudulent, helping financial institutions prevent loss.
   - o **Example**: **MasterCard** uses machine learning to monitor billions of transactions every day, identifying fraudulent activity in real time and notifying customers before they are impacted by fraudulent charges.

3. **Credit Scoring**:
   - o Traditional credit scoring models rely on a limited set of data points, such as credit history and income. However, AI can incorporate a broader range of data, such as purchasing behavior, social media activity, and even phone usage patterns,

to provide a more comprehensive view of an individual's creditworthiness.

- o **Example**: **Zest AI** uses machine learning to create alternative credit scores by analyzing non-traditional data points, enabling more inclusive lending practices. This allows individuals with limited credit histories to access loans they might otherwise be denied.

4. **Algorithmic Trading**:
   - o AI and machine learning are increasingly used in **algorithmic trading**, where algorithms automatically buy and sell financial assets based on predefined criteria. These algorithms can analyze vast amounts of market data, detect trends, and execute trades at high speeds, often making decisions within fractions of a second.
   - o **Example**: **Renaissance Technologies**, a quantitative hedge fund, uses machine learning and AI to create complex trading strategies that analyze market data and execute high-frequency trades, providing them with a competitive edge in the financial markets.

Summary

In this chapter, we explored how **data** serves as the backbone of AI decision-making and its role in driving efficiencies and improvements in work environments across various industries. We also discussed the ethical considerations surrounding **data collection** and **usage**, including privacy concerns, bias in data, and the importance of transparency and consent.

We highlighted **real-world examples** from the **finance industry**, where AI-driven data analysis is revolutionizing risk assessment, fraud detection, credit scoring, and algorithmic trading. As AI continues to integrate into more industries, the ability to responsibly collect, analyze, and use data will be critical in shaping ethical AI systems that benefit society while minimizing harm.

As data continues to be a powerful tool for AI, professionals must navigate the complex balance between harnessing its potential and respecting ethical boundaries, ensuring that data-driven decisions are fair, transparent, and inclusive.

CHAPTER 5

Jobs of the Future: How AI is Creating New Roles

Emerging Job Roles Due to AI Advancements

As AI continues to reshape industries and automate tasks previously done by humans, new job roles are emerging that require a combination of technical skills, creativity, and the ability to work alongside AI systems. These roles are not only focused on developing and managing AI technology, but also on integrating AI into everyday business operations, ensuring its ethical use, and improving how work is performed across all sectors.

1. **AI Specialists and Engineers**:
    - As AI technologies advance, there is an increasing demand for professionals who can develop, train, and maintain AI models. AI specialists, including **machine learning engineers, data scientists**, and **AI researchers**, are crucial for creating the algorithms and systems that power AI.
    - **Example**: A **machine learning engineer** designs and implements models that allow AI to recognize patterns in data, improve over time, and make predictions or decisions based on the data. These engineers are essential for building AI

51

solutions that can be deployed in various industries, from healthcare to finance.

2. **AI Ethicists and Policy Makers**:
   - As AI becomes a more integral part of decision-making processes, ethical concerns regarding its usage, fairness, and transparency have come to the forefront. **AI ethicists** and **policy makers** are emerging as important roles, ensuring that AI systems are used responsibly and align with ethical standards.
   - **Example**: An **AI ethicist** might work within an organization to ensure that the AI systems they develop are free from bias, respect user privacy, and adhere to international ethical guidelines. They are instrumental in shaping policies around data usage and AI deployment in sensitive sectors such as healthcare, finance, and law enforcement.

3. **AI Integration Specialists**:
   - These professionals work to integrate AI technologies into existing business processes, ensuring that AI is used to enhance productivity and efficiency while maintaining human oversight. AI integration specialists bridge the gap between **technical developers** and **end users**, ensuring that AI solutions are implemented effectively and are user-friendly.
   - **Example**: An **AI integration specialist** might work in a **retail company** to

integrate AI-driven customer recommendation systems into the existing sales platform, ensuring a smooth transition and maximizing the impact on sales.

4. **Human-AI Collaboration Experts**:
   - As AI continues to augment human abilities rather than replace workers entirely, there is an increasing demand for professionals who can foster effective collaboration between humans and AI systems. These experts focus on how humans and AI can work together, leveraging the strengths of both.
   - **Example**: A **human-AI collaboration expert** in a **manufacturing environment** might design workflows where AI-powered robots handle repetitive, physically demanding tasks, while humans focus on quality control and complex decision-making, ensuring a harmonious and productive work environment.

5. **AI Trainers and Supervisors**:
   - Many AI systems require ongoing training to remain accurate and up-to-date. AI trainers teach AI models using labeled data, ensuring they continue to perform well over time. Additionally, **AI supervisors** oversee the work performed by AI systems, ensuring that they operate correctly and intervene when human judgment is needed.

o **Example**: An **AI trainer** in the **healthcare sector** might be responsible for labeling medical images to train AI models used in diagnosing diseases. These professionals play a key role in refining AI models and ensuring they remain reliable and effective.

Skills Needed for Future Work Environments

As AI continues to reshape the workforce, it is essential for professionals to develop new skills to stay competitive and thrive in the evolving job market. The skills needed for the future of work will not only include technical expertise in AI but also human-centric skills that enable workers to collaborate effectively with machines.

1. **Technical Skills**:
   o **Machine Learning and Data Science**: A strong understanding of machine learning algorithms, data analysis, and statistical modeling will be essential for many AI-related roles.
   o **Programming Languages**: Proficiency in programming languages such as **Python**, **R**, and **Java** is key for developing and implementing AI models and algorithms.
   o **Big Data**: As AI relies heavily on large datasets, knowledge of **big data tools** (such as **Hadoop** and **Spark**) will be

important for professionals working in AI and data science fields.

2. **Problem-Solving and Critical Thinking**:
   - AI technology may be able to process and analyze vast amounts of data, but humans will continue to play an essential role in interpreting the results, making decisions, and solving complex problems that require human intuition and creativity.
   - Professionals must be able to think critically about the outcomes generated by AI systems and apply their expertise to real-world situations.
   - **Example**: In **financial services**, an AI might predict market trends, but human analysts will be needed to interpret the results and develop actionable strategies based on broader market conditions.

3. **Creativity and Emotional Intelligence**:
   - AI excels at tasks that are rule-based and data-driven, but human creativity and emotional intelligence will remain essential in roles that require innovation, relationship-building, and empathy. Professionals who can leverage AI to complement their creative abilities will have an advantage in industries such as marketing, design, and customer service.
   - **Example**: In **advertising**, AI can optimize ad placements and content delivery, but human marketers are still needed to craft compelling campaigns,

build brand narratives, and understand consumer emotions.

4. **Adaptability and Lifelong Learning**:
   o The rapid pace of technological change means that professionals will need to be adaptable and committed to lifelong learning. Workers who can quickly learn new skills and adapt to new technologies will thrive in AI-driven work environments.
   o **Example**: As **automated tools** are introduced into the healthcare industry, medical professionals must continuously update their knowledge of how to use AI-powered diagnostic tools and integrate them into their clinical practices.

5. **Collaboration with AI**:
   o As AI becomes more integrated into the workplace, professionals will need to develop the ability to collaborate with AI systems effectively. Understanding how AI works, how to communicate with it, and how to leverage its strengths will be vital in ensuring a successful collaboration.
   o **Example**: A **project manager** working with AI-powered scheduling tools must understand the system's capabilities, how to adjust parameters for optimal results, and how to make decisions when the AI produces ambiguous recommendations.

Real-World Example: AI Jobs in Healthcare

The healthcare sector is one of the most dynamic areas where AI is creating new roles and transforming how work is done. AI's ability to process large amounts of medical data, predict health outcomes, and automate routine tasks is improving patient care and streamlining healthcare operations. As AI adoption grows in healthcare, new job roles are emerging to support this transformation.

1. **AI in Medical Diagnostics**:
   o AI algorithms are being used to analyze medical images, such as X-rays, MRIs, and CT scans, to detect diseases like cancer, heart disease, and neurological disorders. These AI systems can identify patterns in medical images with a level of precision that often surpasses human capability.
   o **Example**: A **radiologist AI technician** works with AI-powered diagnostic tools to analyze medical images, helping doctors identify early signs of conditions such as lung cancer, often at stages when human detection is difficult.
2. **AI in Drug Discovery**:
   o AI is revolutionizing drug discovery by analyzing vast datasets of biological and chemical information to identify potential compounds for treating diseases. AI models can predict how different drugs will interact with the human body,

speeding up the development of new treatments and reducing the cost of research.

o **Example**: An **AI-powered drug discovery scientist** might use AI tools to analyze genomic data and identify promising drug candidates, dramatically accelerating the process of finding new treatments for diseases like Alzheimer's or cancer.

3. **AI in Personalized Medicine**:
    o AI is being used to create personalized treatment plans by analyzing a patient's genetic information, medical history, and lifestyle factors. This allows for more tailored treatments that improve patient outcomes and reduce side effects.
    o **Example**: An **AI clinical specialist** works with doctors to design individualized treatment plans for patients based on AI-generated insights derived from their unique genetic and medical data.

4. **AI in Healthcare Administration**:
    o AI is also streamlining healthcare administration by automating tasks like scheduling, patient intake, billing, and insurance claims. This allows healthcare providers to focus more on patient care and less on administrative tasks.
    o **Example**: An **AI-powered healthcare administrator** might use AI tools to optimize hospital schedules, ensuring that

resources are efficiently allocated and patient wait times are minimized.

5. **AI Training and Support Roles**:
   - With the rise of AI-powered healthcare tools, there is also an increased demand for professionals who can train, supervise, and maintain these systems. **AI trainers** ensure that AI models are continuously updated with the latest medical data, while **AI support specialists** help medical staff troubleshoot issues with AI tools.
   - **Example**: An **AI support technician** in a hospital setting ensures that the AI systems used for diagnosing diseases are functioning properly, troubleshooting issues, and ensuring the systems are always up-to-date with the latest medical guidelines.

Summary

In this chapter, we explored how AI is creating new roles in the workforce, as well as the skills that will be required to succeed in an AI-driven work environment. Emerging job roles such as **AI specialists, ethicists, integration experts**, and **human-AI collaboration professionals** are helping to reshape industries. We also discussed how key skills such as **machine learning, critical thinking, creativity**, and **adaptability** will be essential in future workplaces.

A real-world example from **healthcare** highlighted how AI is not only automating tasks like diagnostics and drug discovery but also creating entirely new job roles that require specialized knowledge of both AI and medicine. As AI continues to advance, new job opportunities will emerge, and professionals who can adapt to and collaborate with AI systems will be at the forefront of shaping the future of work.

CHAPTER 6

AI and the Human Workforce: A Symbiotic Relationship

How AI Complements Human Workers

Artificial Intelligence (AI) is often viewed through the lens of disruption, with many fearing that automation and AI will replace human workers. While AI is indeed automating certain tasks, it is also enhancing human capabilities by taking over repetitive, time-consuming, and error-prone tasks, allowing humans to focus on activities that require creativity, problem-solving, and emotional intelligence. The real potential of AI lies not in replacing humans, but in complementing human workers to make them more efficient and effective.

1. **Automating Repetitive Tasks**:
   o AI can handle a range of repetitive tasks that would otherwise take up a significant amount of time for human workers. For example, AI-powered systems can automatically process invoices, sort emails, schedule meetings, and perform data entry, freeing up employees to focus on more strategic, high-value tasks.
   o **Example**: In **customer service**, AI can automate the answering of basic inquiries via chatbots, while human agents handle more complex queries. This not only increases efficiency but also improves job

satisfaction for workers by allowing them to focus on tasks that require more nuanced decision-making.

2. **Enhancing Decision-Making**:
   - o AI can analyze large volumes of data and provide insights that help human workers make more informed decisions. By identifying patterns, trends, and correlations in the data, AI enhances human decision-making by offering evidence-based recommendations and predictions.
   - o **Example**: In **finance**, AI can analyze financial data, market trends, and economic indicators to assist analysts and portfolio managers in making informed investment decisions.

3. **Improving Efficiency**:
   - o AI systems can streamline workflows by identifying bottlenecks and optimizing processes. For instance, in **manufacturing**, AI can track supply chain data in real time and adjust production schedules based on demand, reducing waste and improving efficiency without requiring constant human intervention.
   - o **Example**: **AI-powered robots** in warehouses can optimize order picking and packaging processes, speeding up fulfillment times and reducing errors, allowing human workers to focus on

managing inventory or overseeing more complex tasks.

4. **Providing Personalized Experiences**:
   - AI can help human workers offer more personalized experiences for customers or clients by analyzing data and identifying individual preferences. AI's ability to track and analyze customer interactions enables humans to cater to specific needs, providing more tailored services.
   - **Example**: In **retail**, AI can recommend products to customers based on their browsing history and purchase patterns, but it's the human sales associate who can guide customers in making the final decision based on their unique preferences.

Collaborative Intelligence and Human-AI Partnerships

Rather than replacing human workers, AI is fostering **collaborative intelligence**, where humans and machines work together to leverage their respective strengths. This partnership creates a more powerful and efficient workforce, as AI handles tasks that are data-driven and repetitive, while humans provide creativity, empathy, and critical thinking that AI cannot replicate.

1. **Leveraging AI's Strengths**:
   - AI excels at processing large datasets, identifying patterns, and making predictions based on historical data. It can automate repetitive tasks and analyze data

faster than a human ever could. In contrast, humans excel at tasks that require emotional intelligence, intuition, and decision-making based on ambiguous or incomplete data.

- o **Example**: In **healthcare**, AI can analyze medical imaging to detect early signs of disease, but doctors interpret these results within the context of a patient's history, symptoms, and personal circumstances, making nuanced decisions based on their medical expertise.

2. **Human Expertise Combined with AI Insights**:
   - o In a **human-AI partnership**, human workers bring domain knowledge and expertise to the table, while AI provides data-driven insights and predictive analytics. This combination can lead to more effective and informed decision-making, whether it's in marketing, healthcare, or business strategy.
   - o **Example**: In **advertising**, AI can predict customer behavior and segment audiences, but it's the human marketing expert who determines the most creative messaging and campaign strategy to engage those segments effectively.

3. **Reducing Human Bias**:
   - o AI has the potential to help reduce human bias in decision-making by providing objective data and insights. However, it is important to note that AI models can still carry biases if they are trained on biased

data. Therefore, AI systems must be continuously monitored and tested to ensure fairness and inclusivity.

- ○ **Example**: In **recruitment**, AI tools can analyze resumes or job applicants' past performance data without being influenced by unconscious bias related to gender, ethnicity, or age. However, human recruiters must still oversee the final decisions and ensure that fairness and inclusivity are maintained throughout the process.

4. **Creating New Forms of Work**:
   - ○ As AI automates routine tasks, it enables workers to focus on more fulfilling and higher-value work. This creates the potential for new job roles and career opportunities in industries that previously had limited growth potential due to routine and repetitive tasks. Workers who understand how to collaborate with AI will be better positioned to thrive in this changing landscape.
   - ○ **Example**: In **content creation**, AI can help automate tasks like content curation and SEO optimization, but human writers are still needed to create original, creative content that resonates with audiences.

Real-World Example: AI-Enhanced Customer Support

One of the clearest examples of how AI is complementing human workers is in the **customer**

support industry. AI-powered tools, such as chatbots, virtual assistants, and automated ticketing systems, are revolutionizing the way businesses interact with customers. However, these AI systems are not meant to replace human customer service agents; rather, they work alongside humans to create a more efficient and personalized support experience.

1. **AI Chatbots and Virtual Assistants**:
   - AI-powered chatbots are capable of handling a wide range of customer inquiries, from answering frequently asked questions to assisting with basic account issues. By using natural language processing (NLP), these chatbots can understand and respond to customers in a way that mimics human conversation.
   - **Example**: **Sephora** uses a chatbot called **Sephora Virtual Artist**, which helps customers select makeup products based on their preferences and facial features. This AI-powered assistant enhances the customer experience by providing personalized product recommendations, but human sales associates are still available to answer more complex questions or provide additional guidance.

2. **AI for Ticketing and Issue Resolution**:
   - In customer support centers, AI tools are used to automatically sort, categorize, and prioritize support tickets, directing them to the appropriate department or agent. This helps to ensure that issues are

addressed promptly and efficiently, while human agents can focus on more complex or high-priority issues.

- o **Example**: **Zendesk** utilizes AI to categorize and prioritize customer service tickets, improving response times and ensuring that high-priority tickets are addressed first. While AI handles the sorting and routing of tickets, human agents still handle customer interactions that require empathy and in-depth troubleshooting.

3. **Personalized Customer Interactions**:
   - o AI systems can analyze customer data and previous interactions to create a personalized experience. By predicting customer needs based on past behavior, AI can help customer service agents deliver a more tailored experience, anticipating issues before they arise and offering proactive solutions.
   - o **Example**: **American Express** uses AI to analyze customers' spending habits and provides customer service agents with insights into potential issues or opportunities. This allows agents to offer personalized solutions, such as offering special deals or alerts for upcoming payments, enhancing the overall customer experience.

4. **Human-AI Collaboration**:
   - o Human agents and AI work together to provide a seamless and efficient customer

support experience. While AI handles routine inquiries and tasks, human agents step in to provide nuanced assistance when necessary. This collaboration leads to faster response times and more personalized service, ultimately improving customer satisfaction.

o **Example**: **Lufthansa** uses AI-powered chatbots to assist customers with booking flights, checking flight status, and answering questions about luggage. When customers need more detailed assistance or want to change their flights, human agents are available to handle more complex requests.

Summary

In this chapter, we discussed the **symbiotic relationship** between AI and human workers. Rather than replacing humans, AI is enhancing their abilities by automating routine tasks, improving decision-making, and providing personalized experiences. By leveraging AI's strengths in data processing and pattern recognition, humans can focus on tasks that require creativity, empathy, and complex judgment.

We also explored the concept of **collaborative intelligence**, where AI and humans work together to maximize productivity and innovation. The **real-world example** of **AI-enhanced customer support** illustrated how AI systems like chatbots and virtual assistants complement human customer service agents, creating a more efficient and personalized experience for customers.

As AI continues to evolve, the future of work will depend on how effectively humans and AI can collaborate to achieve shared goals. Professionals who are able to integrate AI into their workflows will be better equipped to handle complex challenges and create innovative solutions, while AI handles the repetitive and data-driven tasks that were once a drain on time and resources.

CHAPTER 7

The Skills Every Professional Needs in the Age of AI

Key Skills for Adapting to the AI-Driven Workforce

As AI continues to transform industries and the nature of work, professionals must develop new skills to stay competitive and thrive in this rapidly evolving landscape. While technical expertise in AI and related technologies is important, a successful career in the age of AI also requires a blend of **soft skills** that complement the capabilities of AI. By adapting to these new demands, workers can ensure that they are not just keeping up with AI but are using it to their advantage.

1. **Technical Skills in AI and Data**:
    o   To remain relevant in an AI-driven workforce, professionals need to develop a strong understanding of AI technologies, such as machine learning, data analysis, and automation. Basic familiarity with **programming languages** like **Python**, **R**, and **Java**, as well as a working knowledge of **data analytics tools**, will be essential for many roles.
    o   **Example**: A **data scientist** needs to have a deep understanding of machine learning algorithms, statistical analysis, and big data tools to design and implement AI

solutions that can extract insights from vast datasets.

2. **Data Literacy**:
   - o In an AI-driven world, understanding how to work with data is a key skill. Data literacy involves the ability to **interpret data**, **evaluate its quality**, and **use it to make informed decisions**. As more industries rely on data-driven insights, professionals will need to be comfortable working with data, even if they are not directly working with AI technologies.
   - o **Example**: A **marketing manager** can use data analysis tools to understand customer behavior, evaluate campaign performance, and tailor strategies based on insights derived from data, even without direct experience in AI.

3. **Problem-Solving and Critical Thinking**:
   - o AI excels at processing large volumes of data, but humans remain best suited for solving complex, ambiguous problems that require creativity, strategic thinking, and the ability to navigate uncertainty. Professionals must develop the ability to approach challenges analytically, break them down into solvable parts, and apply AI insights to come up with innovative solutions.
   - o **Example**: In **healthcare**, while AI can assist with diagnosing diseases from medical images, doctors must still analyze the broader context—patient

history, lifestyle, and symptoms—to determine the most appropriate course of treatment.

4. **Adaptability and Continuous Learning**:
   - The rapid pace of AI advancements requires professionals to remain adaptable and committed to lifelong learning. Those who stay curious and invest in upskilling or reskilling will have the flexibility to navigate changing job roles and industries.
   - **Example**: A **project manager** may need to learn how to use AI-powered project management tools, such as predictive scheduling and resource optimization, to manage teams more efficiently and deliver projects on time.

5. **Collaboration with AI**:
   - As AI continues to work alongside human employees, professionals must understand how to collaborate effectively with AI systems. This involves leveraging AI as a tool to enhance their own work and making the most of its strengths while compensating for areas where human intuition and decision-making are still required.
   - **Example**: A **sales manager** might use an AI-driven customer relationship management (CRM) system to analyze customer data and generate leads. However, the manager must still use their own judgment and experience to

prioritize these leads and develop relationship-building strategies.

6. **Ethical and Responsible Use of AI**:
   - As AI systems are increasingly used in decision-making processes, professionals must be aware of the ethical implications of their work. Understanding the ethical challenges surrounding AI, such as bias, transparency, and fairness, will be crucial in ensuring that AI is used responsibly and does not perpetuate inequality or harm.
   - **Example**: A **HR professional** using AI-powered recruitment tools must be aware of the potential for bias in hiring algorithms and ensure that the tools are used in ways that promote fairness and inclusivity in the hiring process.

Soft Skills vs Technical Skills

In the age of AI, both **soft skills** and **technical skills** are essential for success in the workforce. While technical skills enable workers to interact with AI tools and systems, soft skills are crucial for managing human-AI collaboration, solving complex problems, and navigating the changing work environment.

1. **Technical Skills**:
   - **Hard skills** related to AI and technology, such as programming, data analysis, and machine learning, are essential for roles that involve the development and

management of AI systems. As AI becomes more integrated into business operations, these technical skills will be in high demand across industries.

- o **Example**: A **software engineer** specializing in AI will need a solid understanding of coding languages, data structures, and algorithms to build AI systems that meet specific business needs.

2. **Soft Skills**:
   - o While technical skills are important, **soft skills**—such as emotional intelligence, communication, creativity, and critical thinking—will be equally valuable. Soft skills enable individuals to collaborate with AI systems, interact effectively with colleagues, and navigate the complex ethical, societal, and organizational challenges that AI presents.
   - o **Example**: A **team leader** must have strong communication skills to effectively manage a diverse team, integrate AI tools into workflows, and foster collaboration between human workers and AI systems.

3. **The Complementary Nature of Soft and Technical Skills**:
   - o In the AI-driven workforce, the best-performing professionals will be those who combine technical expertise with strong interpersonal skills. For example, a **data scientist** with great technical knowledge may excel at building machine

learning models, but their ability to communicate insights to non-technical stakeholders and collaborate with other teams will significantly enhance their impact.

- o **Example**: A **healthcare data analyst** needs to analyze patient data using AI tools, but they must also explain their findings in a way that is understandable to medical professionals, ensuring that AI insights are integrated into treatment decisions.

Real-World Example: Upskilling Programs in Tech Companies

As AI and other technologies rapidly evolve, companies are recognizing the importance of investing in upskilling and reskilling programs for their employees. These programs ensure that workers have the skills needed to work effectively alongside AI and stay competitive in the changing job market.

1. **Tech Giants and Upskilling**:
   - o Many tech companies have launched extensive **upskilling programs** to help their employees adapt to the increasing presence of AI. These programs offer training in AI technologies, data science, programming, and other relevant fields, giving employees the tools to succeed in an AI-enhanced workplace.

- o **Example**: **Google's AI Residency Program** is designed to train engineers in machine learning and AI research, offering them hands-on experience working with Google's AI teams. This program allows employees to deepen their expertise and stay current with the latest advancements in AI.

2. **Corporate Training Initiatives**:
   - o Companies across industries are providing their employees with access to online courses, certifications, and workshops that focus on AI and related technologies. By partnering with educational platforms like **Coursera** and **Udacity**, businesses are helping workers build both technical and soft skills.
   - o **Example**: **Accenture** offers AI-focused upskilling programs to its employees, enabling them to build the skills necessary to implement AI solutions for clients. These programs cover AI ethics, data science, and machine learning, helping employees stay relevant in an AI-driven business environment.

3. **Reskilling Programs for Career Transition**:
   - o As AI and automation reshape industries, many companies are also offering **reskilling programs** to help employees transition into new roles that leverage their existing skills while developing new ones. These programs help workers navigate job displacement and equip them

with the knowledge needed to thrive in evolving industries.

- o **Example**: **Amazon** has invested heavily in upskilling its workforce, offering programs like **Amazon Web Services (AWS) Training and Certification** to teach employees cloud computing and machine learning, helping them transition into new roles within the company as technology continues to advance.

4. **Partnerships with Universities and Institutions**:
   - o Companies are increasingly collaborating with universities and educational institutions to create tailored upskilling programs that meet the needs of their workforce. These partnerships ensure that employees receive high-quality, relevant training that aligns with the demands of the AI-driven job market.
   - o **Example**: **IBM** has partnered with several universities to offer AI-focused certifications and degree programs, providing students and professionals with the skills needed to succeed in the AI field. IBM's **AI Skills Academy** focuses on training the next generation of AI professionals and ensuring that they have the skills needed for future job roles.

Summary

In this chapter, we explored the essential skills needed for professionals to adapt and thrive in the **AI-driven workforce**. We discussed the importance of both **technical skills**—such as machine learning, data science, and programming—and **soft skills**, such as communication, problem-solving, creativity, and emotional intelligence. As AI continues to evolve, the best professionals will be those who can blend these skills to work alongside AI systems, making informed decisions and fostering collaboration between humans and machines.

We also highlighted real-world examples of **upskilling programs** in **tech companies** like **Google**, **Amazon**, and **IBM**, which are helping employees stay competitive by providing them with the knowledge and tools necessary to succeed in an AI-driven world. These initiatives focus on developing both technical expertise and soft skills, ensuring that employees are well-equipped to navigate the evolving job landscape and continue to thrive in the age of AI.

CHAPTER 8

AI and the Gig Economy: Transforming Freelance Work

The Rise of AI in the Gig Economy

The **gig economy** has seen explosive growth in recent years, fueled by technological advancements that make it easier for individuals to work on a flexible, short-term basis. Freelance and contract work is now a common way of life for millions, with platforms like **Uber**, **Airbnb**, and **Upwork** creating vast networks for gig workers to connect with clients. In this evolving landscape, **Artificial Intelligence (AI)** is playing a key role in transforming how freelance work is conducted, making the process of finding gigs, managing projects, and receiving payment faster and more efficient.

1. **AI's Role in the Gig Economy**:
    o AI technologies such as **machine learning**, **data analytics**, and **automation** are streamlining the gig economy by providing intelligent matchmaking between freelancers and clients. AI systems can now predict a freelancer's performance based on their past work and suggest relevant jobs or projects, making it easier for both parties to find the right fit.
    o **Example**: On platforms like **Upwork** or **Fiverr**, AI algorithms recommend job

opportunities based on a freelancer's skillset, previous work history, and client ratings, allowing them to find gigs that match their strengths.

2. **AI-Powered Job Matching**:
   - One of the most significant ways AI is transforming the gig economy is through **job matching**. Traditionally, finding the right freelancer for a job involved a lot of manual searching and screening. AI can now analyze large datasets to recommend the best freelancers for a particular project, using criteria such as skills, previous work experience, client feedback, and job performance.
   - **Example**: AI-powered platforms like **Toptal** use algorithms to match highly skilled freelancers with clients seeking specific expertise in areas like **software development**, **finance**, or **design**. The AI ensures that only the most qualified candidates are recommended, optimizing the hiring process for clients.

3. **Automation of Administrative Tasks**:
   - Freelancers often face administrative burdens, such as invoicing, time tracking, and tax calculations. AI tools are automating these routine tasks, giving freelancers more time to focus on their core work. Freelancers can now use AI-powered tools to generate invoices, track time, and even handle tax filing automatically.

- o **Example**: **Harvest** and **Toggl** are time-tracking platforms that use AI to automatically record hours worked on different projects, generate invoices, and integrate with other accounting tools. This automation simplifies workflow management, reducing administrative headaches for freelancers.

4. **AI for Project Management and Collaboration**:
   - o AI is improving project management for freelancers by automating scheduling, task management, and collaboration. Freelancers working on larger projects or in teams can benefit from AI tools that optimize workflows, track progress, and provide real-time feedback on project status.
   - o **Example**: Tools like **Asana** and **Trello**, which are popular in team environments, are integrating AI features to help freelancers manage their tasks more effectively. AI can suggest tasks based on project deadlines or workload, ensuring that freelancers stay on track and meet client expectations.

How AI is Reshaping Freelance Work

The use of AI in the gig economy is not only making freelance work more efficient but also reshaping the way freelancers manage their careers. AI is enabling freelancers to be more self-sufficient, with tools that allow them to find jobs, manage projects, and even learn new skills—without relying on traditional employment structures.

1. **Skill Development and Learning**:
   - o Freelancers are often required to keep their skills up-to-date to remain competitive in an ever-changing market. AI is supporting continuous learning by providing personalized recommendations for courses, tutorials, and certifications based on a freelancer's career goals and past performance.
   - o **Example**: **LinkedIn Learning**, powered by AI, offers personalized skill-building recommendations for freelancers, helping them stay competitive in their industries. By analyzing trends in job postings and identifying emerging skills, AI can help freelancers predict what skills will be in high demand in the future.
2. **Increasing Access to Global Clients**:
   - o One of the key advantages of freelance work is the ability to serve clients across the world. AI is making it easier for freelancers to connect with global clients, removing barriers related to time zones, language, and location. AI-powered translation tools and communication platforms make it simpler to work with clients from different countries and cultures.

- o **Example**: **Freelancer.com** uses AI to translate project descriptions, allowing clients and freelancers to work together seamlessly despite language differences. This opens up a broader market for freelancers, enabling them to access a global client base.

3. **Dynamic Pricing Models**:
   - o AI is also helping freelancers set competitive pricing for their services by analyzing data from similar freelancers, projects, and industries. Machine learning algorithms can provide recommendations on how to price services based on factors like experience, expertise, project complexity, and market demand.
   - o **Example**: **Freelancer.com** and **Upwork** have integrated AI-powered pricing tools that suggest pricing based on a freelancer's skills, location, and job history. This ensures freelancers remain competitive while maximizing their earnings.

4. **Improved Job Security and Stability**:
   - o Freelancers often face uncertainty regarding job security and the consistency of their income. AI-driven platforms are working to address this by predicting demand for freelance work and providing data-driven insights on which sectors are hiring the most. Freelancers can use these insights to target their efforts more effectively and find long-term projects.

- o **Example**: **Upwork's "Rising Talent"** feature leverages AI to identify freelancers with high potential based on their job history, client feedback, and skills. These freelancers are more likely to be recommended for long-term, high-paying projects, creating a more stable career path in the gig economy.

5. **AI for Freelance Community Building**:
    - o Freelancers often work in isolation, lacking the collaborative environment that traditional office jobs provide. AI is helping to build virtual communities for freelancers, where they can collaborate, share insights, and network with peers. These platforms offer AI-driven suggestions for collaboration, idea-sharing, and even socializing.
    - o **Example**: **Fiverr** provides a **community platform** where freelancers can discuss their experiences, share resources, and collaborate on projects. AI-powered algorithms suggest relevant groups or forums based on a freelancer's niche, fostering a sense of community within the gig economy.

Real-World Example: AI Platforms for Freelance Workers

Several AI-driven platforms have emerged in recent years that specifically cater to freelancers, leveraging AI to streamline job matching, enhance productivity, and foster collaboration. These platforms are transforming the gig economy by giving freelancers the tools they need to succeed in a competitive landscape.

1. **Upwork**:
   - **Upwork** is one of the largest freelancing platforms, connecting freelancers with clients around the world. The platform uses AI to recommend jobs to freelancers based on their skillset, work history, and ratings. AI also helps clients find the best freelancers by analyzing data on past projects, client feedback, and freelancer expertise.
   - **Example**: An AI-powered feature on **Upwork** suggests relevant projects to freelancers based on their previous work experience, helping them find the best opportunities without having to constantly search for new gigs.

2. **Fiverr**:
   - **Fiverr** is another popular platform for freelancers, particularly in creative fields like graphic design, writing, and web development. AI is used to match freelancers with clients based on project descriptions, skills, and portfolio reviews. The platform also uses AI to predict which freelancers are likely to get hired, boosting their visibility.
   - **Example**: **Fiverr's AI-powered algorithm** analyzes the work history and client reviews of freelancers to promote

the most successful freelancers for new job postings, helping them stand out and secure more work.

3. **Freelancer.com**:
   - **Freelancer.com** uses AI-driven job matching to pair clients with freelancers who possess the right skills and experience. The platform uses machine learning to analyze project details and freelancer profiles, ensuring that both parties are matched effectively and efficiently. It also employs AI for payment processing, ensuring smooth financial transactions between clients and freelancers.
   - **Example: Freelancer.com's AI system** automates the bidding process, allowing freelancers to be matched with projects that suit their expertise. AI also assists in predicting the likelihood of a job being awarded, helping freelancers prioritize their efforts.

4. **Toptal**:
   - **Toptal** is a highly curated platform that connects top-tier freelancers with clients in need of specialized skills. The platform uses AI to identify highly skilled freelancers based on an in-depth evaluation process, ensuring that only the best talent is recommended to clients.
   - **Example**: **Toptal's AI-powered algorithm** selects freelancers based on a rigorous screening process, analyzing

factors such as technical proficiency, problem-solving ability, and previous work history. This ensures that clients have access to the highest quality talent in fields like software development, design, and finance.

Summary

In this chapter, we explored how **AI is transforming the gig economy**, from streamlining job matching and project management to enhancing freelancers' access to global opportunities. AI platforms are empowering freelancers by automating repetitive tasks, recommending jobs, and improving the efficiency of administrative processes. These changes are creating a more dynamic, flexible, and competitive freelance landscape, where freelancers can focus on higher-value work and more personalized client interactions.

We also looked at real-world examples of AI-driven freelance platforms such as **Upwork**, **Fiverr**, **Freelancer.com**, and **Toptal**, which use AI to match freelancers with clients, predict job demand, and foster better collaboration. As the gig economy continues to expand, AI is playing a crucial role in shaping how freelancers work, manage their careers, and adapt to new opportunities. Freelancers who embrace AI tools and technologies will have a competitive edge in the evolving workforce, positioning themselves for long-term success in the age of automation.

CHAPTER 9

The Ethical Implications of AI in the Workplace

Ethical Challenges Posed by AI in Professional Settings

As AI becomes more prevalent in the workplace, it brings with it a range of **ethical challenges** that need to be carefully considered. While AI can offer incredible efficiencies and improve decision-making, its implementation in professional settings raises concerns about fairness, transparency, accountability, and the potential for unintended consequences.

1. **Privacy and Surveillance**:
    - **AI systems** often collect, process, and analyze large amounts of personal data. In the workplace, this can lead to ethical concerns about employee **privacy**. AI tools used for monitoring productivity, communication, or even physical activity (e.g., through sensors) can encroach on personal space and create a sense of constant surveillance, which can negatively impact morale.
    - **Example**: AI-driven **employee surveillance systems** that track keystrokes, emails, or even facial expressions during meetings can raise significant concerns about privacy and the ethical limits of workplace monitoring.
2. **Accountability and Transparency**:

- o AI systems often operate as "black boxes" where the decision-making process is opaque. This lack of **transparency** makes it difficult to understand how AI arrives at its decisions and poses challenges when outcomes are disputed or unfair. Determining who is accountable for the decisions made by AI systems—whether it's the software developer, the company, or the AI itself—can be difficult.
- o **Example**: In a **customer service setting**, if an AI chatbot provides an incorrect or harmful response, who is responsible— the company using the bot, the developers, or the AI system itself?

3. **Autonomy and Job Displacement**:
   - o One of the most talked-about ethical challenges of AI in the workplace is its potential to displace jobs. As AI automates tasks previously performed by humans, there are concerns about workers losing their livelihoods, especially in sectors that rely on manual or repetitive labor.
   - o **Example**: In **manufacturing**, robots and AI systems are increasingly used for tasks like assembly, quality control, and inventory management. While these systems increase efficiency, they also displace human workers, raising concerns about job loss and the ethical responsibility of companies to retrain their workforce.

4. **AI Decision-Making and Human Oversight**:
   - o The use of AI in **decision-making** processes—such as hiring, promotions, or performance evaluations—can lead to situations where important decisions are made without human oversight or intervention. The reliance on AI for critical decisions may overlook human factors like empathy, intuition, or the nuances of personal context.
   - o **Example**: In **hiring processes**, an AI system might reject a candidate based on a set of patterns it identifies in resumes, without considering the broader context of an applicant's qualifications, experiences, or personal situation.

Addressing Bias, Discrimination, and Fairness in AI

As AI becomes increasingly integrated into workplace decision-making processes, there are growing concerns about its potential to perpetuate or even exacerbate **bias**, **discrimination**, and **inequality**. Since AI systems learn from data, any biases present in the data can be mirrored and magnified by AI, leading to unfair outcomes for certain groups of people.

1. **Bias in AI Systems**:
   - o **Bias in AI** occurs when algorithms produce unfair, prejudiced, or skewed results due to the data used to train them. This can happen if the data used to train AI models reflects historical prejudices or

unequal distributions (e.g., gender, racial, or socioeconomic bias).

- o **Example**: A facial recognition AI trained primarily on light-skinned faces may perform poorly when identifying darker-skinned individuals, leading to unequal treatment and discrimination.

2. **Algorithmic Bias and Its Consequences**:
   - o AI systems are only as unbiased as the data they are trained on. If biased data is used, AI systems will perpetuate these biases. This can have serious consequences, especially when AI is used in sensitive decision-making processes, such as hiring, criminal justice, and lending.
   - o **Example**: In **criminal justice**, AI systems used for risk assessments in sentencing or parole decisions may be trained on biased data that disproportionately targets minority groups, leading to racial profiling or unfair treatment of certain populations.

3. **Ensuring Fairness**:
   - o Ensuring fairness in AI systems involves recognizing and mitigating biases in the data, ensuring equal representation of various groups, and implementing mechanisms for transparency and accountability. Fairness also means ensuring that AI decisions do not disproportionately harm one group or favor another, and that there are avenues

for individuals to challenge decisions made by AI systems.

- o **Example**: Companies can use **bias detection tools** to audit their AI systems regularly and ensure they do not make discriminatory decisions. **Fairness constraints** can be implemented in the training process to prevent biased outcomes, and diverse datasets can be used to improve the performance of AI systems across various demographic groups.

4. **Inclusive AI Design**:
   - o To combat bias, AI systems need to be designed with inclusivity in mind. This means incorporating **diverse perspectives** during the development and deployment phases of AI, as well as ensuring that the data used is representative of all groups.
   - o **Example**: When developing **AI in healthcare**, including data from diverse populations, such as different age groups, ethnicities, and genders, can help create more equitable healthcare solutions that work for everyone, not just the majority.

5. **The Role of Human Oversight**:
   - o While AI can be an invaluable tool for decision-making, human oversight remains crucial in ensuring that decisions are ethical and fair. Humans need to continuously monitor AI systems, evaluate their outputs, and intervene

when necessary to prevent harmful or biased decisions.
- o **Example**: In **hiring**, while AI can assist in screening candidates, human recruiters should ensure that final hiring decisions are made with careful consideration of context and fairness, and that biases in the AI's recommendations are identified and addressed.

Real-World Example: AI in Hiring and Recruitment Processes

One of the most common applications of AI in the workplace is in **hiring and recruitment**. AI-powered tools are increasingly used to screen resumes, assess candidates, and even conduct initial interviews. While these systems can help companies streamline their hiring processes and reduce costs, they also raise significant ethical concerns regarding fairness, bias, and transparency.

1. **Resume Screening and Candidate Evaluation**:
   - o Many companies use **AI algorithms** to screen resumes, rank candidates, and identify top talent. These AI systems analyze resumes for keywords, skills, and past experiences, allowing recruiters to quickly sift through large volumes of applicants.
   - o **Example**: **HireVue**, a recruitment platform, uses AI to analyze video interviews, assessing candidates' facial

expressions, tone of voice, and speech patterns to evaluate their suitability for a job. However, there are concerns that these algorithms may inadvertently favor candidates who fit certain **demographic profiles**, leading to biased outcomes.

2. **Bias in AI Recruitment Tools**:
   - AI recruitment tools can unintentionally perpetuate biases if they are trained on biased data. For example, if the AI system is trained using historical hiring data from a company that has predominantly hired male candidates, the AI may favor male candidates over female candidates, or even discriminate against other underrepresented groups.
   - **Example**: In 2018, **Amazon** abandoned an AI recruitment tool that was found to be biased against female candidates. The system had been trained on resumes submitted to Amazon over a 10-year period, which were mostly from male applicants, leading the AI to favor resumes from men over women.

3. **Addressing Bias in AI Recruitment**:
   - Companies must take proactive steps to address bias in AI recruitment tools. This includes using diverse and representative datasets to train AI systems, regularly auditing AI tools for fairness, and incorporating human oversight into the final decision-making process.

- ○ **Example**: To mitigate bias, **Unilever** revamped its AI recruitment process by using an AI system that helps screen candidates based on cognitive and emotional traits, rather than traditional resume criteria. They also implemented a more diverse team of developers to ensure that the AI tool was fair and inclusive.

4. **Ensuring Transparency and Accountability**:
   - ○ Transparency is essential in AI-driven recruitment processes. Job applicants must understand how AI systems are being used to evaluate them and should have access to information about how decisions are made. In addition, companies must be accountable for the outcomes of AI decisions, especially when they impact hiring or promotion opportunities.
   - ○ **Example**: **IBM Watson** offers a **transparency report** that outlines how its AI recruitment tools make decisions and encourages companies to adopt transparent practices that allow applicants to understand the algorithms behind their hiring decisions.

5. **Human Intervention and Final Decision-Making**:
   - ○ While AI can assist with resume screening and initial candidate evaluation, human recruiters should always have the final say in hiring decisions. Human oversight ensures that AI's

recommendations are tempered with context, empathy, and understanding of the unique circumstances of each candidate.

- ○ **Example**: In **Google's hiring process**, AI is used to recommend candidates for interviews based on resumes and previous performance, but final interview decisions are made by human hiring managers who can evaluate candidates in person and ensure fairness.

Summary

In this chapter, we examined the **ethical implications of AI in the workplace**, highlighting challenges related to **privacy**, **transparency**, **bias**, and **accountability**. As AI continues to automate and assist in decision-making, it is crucial that businesses consider the ethical ramifications of their AI systems, ensuring that they are used fairly and transparently.

We explored how **bias** in AI, particularly in areas like **recruitment**, can perpetuate discrimination if not properly addressed. By using diverse data, ensuring transparency, and maintaining human oversight, companies can mitigate these risks and create more equitable AI systems.

A **real-world example** from **AI in hiring** demonstrated how AI-powered recruitment tools can both benefit and challenge ethical practices. While AI can help streamline recruitment and reduce bias in certain cases, it can also inadvertently reinforce discrimination if not carefully monitored. As AI becomes increasingly integrated into workplace processes, it is essential to prioritize ethical considerations to ensure that AI benefits all individuals equally and fairly.

CHAPTER 10

Managing Change in the Workplace: AI and Organizational Culture

How Organizations Can Adapt to AI Technology

As AI technology continues to evolve, it presents both opportunities and challenges for organizations across industries. While AI promises to boost efficiency, enhance decision-making, and automate repetitive tasks, its integration into an organization's workflow requires significant changes. For organizations to thrive in an AI-driven landscape, they must be willing to adapt to new ways of working, restructure business processes, and embrace a mindset of continuous learning and innovation.

1. **Understanding the Impact of AI**:
    o Before adopting AI, organizations must first understand how the technology will impact their existing processes, workflows, and culture. This includes identifying areas where AI can provide the most value, whether by automating tasks, improving data analysis, or enhancing customer interactions. A clear understanding of AI's potential helps businesses create a roadmap for successful implementation.

- o **Example**: An **e-commerce company** might identify customer service, inventory management, and personalized recommendations as key areas where AI can add value. The company's leadership would then plan how to integrate AI systems into these processes and allocate resources for implementation.

2. **Building AI Competence Within the Organization**:
   - o For AI adoption to be successful, organizations must ensure that their teams possess the necessary skills and knowledge to work with AI tools effectively. This includes investing in training programs to upskill employees and helping them understand how AI can augment their roles.
   - o **Example**: A **banking institution** could offer training in **machine learning** and **data science** for their analysts, so they are better equipped to work with AI-powered financial tools that assist in credit scoring or fraud detection.

3. **Fostering a Culture of Innovation and Continuous Learning**:
   - o AI technology evolves rapidly, so organizations must foster a culture that values **innovation**, **adaptability**, and **continuous learning**. Encouraging employees to embrace AI and explore how it can improve their work fosters a more dynamic, forward-thinking culture.

o **Example**: A **tech company** may hold regular **hackathons** or **innovation days**, encouraging employees to experiment with new AI tools, share ideas, and explore ways to incorporate AI into their work processes.

4. **Strategic Implementation of AI**:

o When implementing AI, it is crucial for organizations to take a **strategic, phased approach**. Starting with pilot projects, collecting feedback, and gradually scaling the technology helps organizations avoid large-scale failures and ensures smoother integration.

o **Example**: A **manufacturing company** might start with a pilot project to automate its inventory management using AI. Once the technology is proven to increase efficiency and reduce errors, the company can expand AI implementation to other departments, such as predictive maintenance or quality control.

The Role of Leadership in AI Adoption

Effective leadership is essential for AI adoption in organizations. Leaders play a critical role in guiding the organization through the change process, setting a clear vision for AI implementation, and ensuring that the workforce is aligned with the organization's goals. Leadership also sets the tone for embracing innovation and ensuring that AI is integrated ethically and responsibly.

1. **Setting the Vision and Strategy**:
   o Leaders must communicate a clear vision for AI adoption, demonstrating how it aligns with the organization's broader goals and values. This vision should encompass the strategic goals of the organization and identify the areas where AI will have the most significant impact.
   o **Example**: In a **healthcare organization**, leadership may set the vision of using AI to improve patient care and optimize resource allocation. By aligning AI adoption with the organization's mission of delivering high-quality healthcare, leadership ensures that AI initiatives support the broader goals.
2. **Championing Change and Overcoming Resistance**:
   o AI adoption often faces resistance from employees who fear job displacement or struggle with new technologies. Leadership plays an important role in addressing these concerns by promoting a culture of collaboration and reassuring employees that AI is a tool to complement their work, not replace it.
   o **Example**: A **retail chain** implementing AI-powered inventory management systems might face resistance from employees worried about job loss. Leaders can overcome this resistance by emphasizing how AI will enable employees to focus on higher-value tasks,

such as customer service, while AI handles the more mundane inventory tasks.

3. **Investing in Talent and Resources**:
   - o For AI initiatives to succeed, leaders must invest in both the **right talent** and the **necessary resources**. This includes hiring AI specialists, providing ongoing training for existing employees, and ensuring that the organization has the technology infrastructure to support AI tools.
   - o **Example**: A **financial services firm** looking to implement AI-based fraud detection might hire data scientists and machine learning engineers to build and deploy the models, while also offering ongoing training for existing staff to adapt to AI-enhanced workflows.

4. **Ethical Leadership in AI Adoption**:
   - o Leaders must also ensure that AI systems are implemented ethically and responsibly, considering potential biases, data privacy concerns, and the impact of AI on employees. Ethical leadership involves guiding the organization to adopt AI technologies that prioritize fairness, transparency, and accountability.
   - o **Example**: A **law firm** implementing AI to assist with legal research must ensure that the AI system is free from bias, transparent in its decision-making

processes, and designed to respect client confidentiality and privacy.

Real-World Example: AI Implementation in a Traditional Office Setting

Implementing AI in a traditional office setting presents unique challenges. Office environments often rely on legacy systems and established workflows, making it harder to integrate new technologies like AI. However, with the right approach, AI can dramatically enhance productivity, improve collaboration, and drive innovation within the workplace.

1. **Automation of Routine Office Tasks**:
   - One of the first areas where AI can be integrated into a traditional office environment is in the automation of routine tasks. AI can handle repetitive administrative functions such as scheduling, data entry, email sorting, and document management. This frees up human employees to focus on more strategic, high-level tasks.
   - **Example**: A **corporate law firm** might use AI to automate contract review and legal research. AI-powered tools can quickly scan contracts for key clauses and identify potential risks, saving lawyers significant time in reviewing documents.
2. **AI in Document Management and Collaboration**:

- o AI-powered document management systems can help organize, categorize, and retrieve files more efficiently. These systems can also assist with collaboration by automatically tagging documents, suggesting relevant content, and streamlining workflows.
- o **Example**: **Microsoft 365**'s **AI-powered productivity tools** help office workers by automatically organizing emails, suggesting responses, and assisting with task prioritization. This helps employees save time on administrative work, allowing them to focus on higher-value tasks like client relationships and business strategy.

3. **AI for Enhanced Communication and Customer Support**:
   - o AI can also improve communication both within the organization and with clients. Virtual assistants, chatbots, and AI-enhanced communication tools can facilitate smoother workflows, enabling employees to find information faster and respond to queries more efficiently.
   - o **Example**: **Zendesk's AI-powered customer service platform** can automatically route customer queries to the appropriate department and suggest responses, allowing customer support teams to manage higher volumes of tickets and resolve issues faster.

4. **Performance and Productivity Tracking**:

- o AI can track employee productivity and performance, offering insights into how work is being done and identifying potential bottlenecks or areas for improvement. By using AI to monitor performance, organizations can make data-driven decisions to optimize workflows.
- o **Example**: A **project management company** might use AI to track the progress of various projects, automatically adjusting timelines and resource allocations based on real-time data. This allows managers to make more informed decisions and improve project outcomes.

5. **AI-Powered Decision Support**:
- o AI can also support decision-making in a traditional office environment by analyzing data, generating insights, and recommending actions. AI-powered analytics can help leaders make more informed decisions based on real-time data, leading to better outcomes for the organization.
- o **Example**: A **marketing agency** could use AI to analyze customer behavior, segment audiences, and predict the success of different marketing campaigns, empowering employees to make more data-driven marketing decisions.

Summary

In this chapter, we explored the role of **AI in transforming organizational culture** and adapting to an AI-driven workplace. We discussed how organizations can strategically adopt AI by understanding its impact, building AI competence, and fostering a culture of innovation. The role of **leadership** is crucial in ensuring the successful adoption of AI, from setting a clear vision to investing in resources and maintaining ethical practices throughout the implementation process.

We also examined **real-world examples** of AI implementation in **traditional office settings**, where AI is automating routine tasks, enhancing communication, improving decision-making, and boosting productivity. By leveraging AI technologies in a thoughtful and strategic way, organizations can enhance their operations, create more efficient workflows, and empower employees to focus on higher-value, creative tasks.

As AI continues to evolve, organizations must prioritize both **technological innovation** and **cultural transformation** to ensure that they can adapt successfully to the changing workplace. Leaders must guide their teams through the complexities of AI adoption, fostering a culture that embraces technology while ensuring fairness, transparency, and ethical practices.

CHAPTER 11

AI and Remote Work: The New Normal

How AI is Enabling and Supporting Remote Work

The COVID-19 pandemic accelerated the adoption of **remote work**, and now, **AI** is playing a significant role in shaping the future of this work model. Remote work presents unique challenges, such as communication barriers, time zone differences, and managing productivity from a distance. However, AI technologies are providing effective solutions to these problems by enhancing collaboration, automating tasks, and supporting employees in managing their work in a distributed environment.

1. **AI-Powered Communication**:
   - One of the key challenges of remote work is maintaining effective communication across teams that are physically dispersed. AI-powered communication tools can help bridge these gaps by providing real-time translation, automatic transcription, and even sentiment analysis to ensure that messages are understood and team dynamics are positive.
   - **Example**: **Google Meet** and **Zoom** offer real-time **captioning** and **language translation** features powered by AI, which help facilitate communication

between team members who speak different languages, enhancing inclusivity and reducing misunderstandings in virtual meetings.

2. **AI in Time and Task Management**:

   o Remote workers often struggle with managing their time and tasks effectively due to distractions or a lack of structure. AI tools can assist by automatically tracking time, managing schedules, setting reminders, and even suggesting the most productive times for working based on past performance.

   o **Example**: **Time-tracking tools** like **RescueTime** or **Clockify** use AI to analyze how employees spend their time on tasks and websites, offering insights into productivity and helping employees stay on track without manual tracking.

3. **AI for Personalizing Workflows**:

   o AI can analyze an employee's past behavior and work habits to create personalized workflows, making remote work more efficient. These tools can help workers automate mundane tasks like scheduling, email management, and document organization, allowing them to focus on more complex, creative work.

   o **Example**: AI-powered **email management** tools like **SaneBox** use machine learning to filter important emails and prioritize tasks, automatically sorting incoming messages based on urgency and relevance, reducing email overload for remote workers.

4. **Predictive Analytics for Remote Work Trends**:
   o AI can use data analytics to predict future work trends, offering businesses the ability to proactively adapt to remote work challenges. By analyzing historical data, AI can help organizations forecast project timelines, identify potential bottlenecks, and optimize resource allocation for remote teams.
   o **Example**: **Monday.com** and **Trello** use AI to predict project completion times, allocate resources efficiently, and highlight potential delays, ensuring that remote teams stay aligned and on schedule.

Tools for Managing Remote Teams with AI

Managing remote teams requires effective coordination, communication, and collaboration. AI-powered tools help leaders monitor team performance, provide feedback, and ensure that employees have the support they need to succeed in a remote work environment.

1. **AI-Powered Project Management Tools**:
   o **Project management tools** powered by AI can help organize tasks, set deadlines, and track team progress. These tools automate project timelines, allocate tasks based on team members' skillsets, and

adjust schedules as needed to keep remote teams on track.

- o **Example**: **Asana** and **ClickUp** use AI to automate task assignments, manage deadlines, and track project progress. AI-based features like **task dependencies** and **timeline suggestions** ensure that remote teams stay organized, even when working on complex projects.

2. **AI for Performance Tracking and Feedback**:
   - o AI can provide real-time performance tracking and feedback, offering insights into individual and team productivity. It can also track how often employees interact with colleagues, the quality of their work, and how effectively they manage their time, enabling managers to provide personalized support.
   - o **Example**: **15Five**, an employee engagement tool, uses AI to measure employee satisfaction, productivity, and performance. The platform's AI capabilities also help managers identify areas where team members may need additional support or training, improving both individual and team performance.

3. **AI-Based Virtual Assistants for Remote Teams**:
   - o Virtual assistants powered by AI can help remote teams manage their schedules, answer frequently asked questions, and automate repetitive administrative tasks. By acting as a personal assistant, AI can

make it easier for remote workers to stay focused on their work without getting bogged down by small, time-consuming tasks.

- **Example**: **Slack** has integrated AI-powered **Slackbot**, which helps teams automate simple tasks like setting reminders, answering common questions, and managing team workflows, allowing employees to focus on higher-level tasks.

4. **AI for Employee Wellness**:
   - AI can be used to monitor and support the **well-being** of remote workers. AI tools can track signs of burnout, analyze patterns in work habits, and suggest breaks, exercises, or wellness tips based on individual work habits and health data.
   - **Example**: **Humu** is an AI-powered platform that helps organizations track employee happiness, engagement, and mental health. By analyzing feedback and behavioral patterns, the system provides personalized recommendations for boosting employee morale and well-being, ensuring that remote workers stay healthy and productive.

Real-World Example: AI-Powered Remote Collaboration Tools

Several companies and platforms have embraced AI-powered tools to make remote collaboration easier and more effective. These tools help remote teams stay connected, improve communication, and enhance productivity, despite the physical distance between team members.

1. **Microsoft Teams and AI-Powered Collaboration**:
   - o **Microsoft Teams** is a widely used collaboration platform that integrates AI features to enhance remote work. It includes tools for virtual meetings, file sharing, project collaboration, and more. AI features such as real-time transcription, voice recognition, and automated scheduling help improve communication and ensure that remote teams stay productive.
   - o **Example**: Teams uses AI for **transcriptions** and **translation** during meetings, ensuring that everyone, regardless of language or location, can participate equally in real-time conversations. AI also automatically organizes meeting summaries and action points for teams to review after meetings, making it easier to track progress and follow through on tasks.
2. **Zoom and AI-Enhanced Virtual Meetings**:
   - o **Zoom** has been at the forefront of remote communication, integrating AI features to improve video conferencing and collaboration. AI-powered features such as **background noise suppression**, **virtual backgrounds**, and **automatic**

meeting summaries enhance the virtual meeting experience for remote teams.

- o **Example**: **Zoom's AI** automatically adjusts video quality based on network conditions, ensuring that remote teams have a stable and seamless meeting experience, even when working from locations with limited internet connectivity.

3. **Trello and AI-Powered Task Management**:
   - o **Trello**, a popular project management tool, has incorporated AI features to help remote teams organize and track their work more efficiently. With its **AI-powered automation**, Trello allows team members to automate workflows, set task reminders, and update project statuses, reducing the need for manual updates and improving team collaboration.
   - o **Example**: **Butler**, an AI-powered automation tool within Trello, automatically assigns tasks, sets due dates, and sends notifications, keeping remote teams aligned without needing constant manual intervention.

4. **Miro and Collaborative Whiteboarding**:
   - o **Miro** is a virtual whiteboard platform that enables remote teams to collaborate on creative projects. With AI-enhanced features, Miro helps teams brainstorm, plan, and visualize ideas in real time, making it easier for remote workers to

work together on creative projects despite being in different locations.

- o **Example**: Miro's **AI-based suggestions** help facilitate collaborative brainstorming sessions by recommending templates, tools, or frameworks that are relevant to the team's current project, making remote teamwork more efficient and productive.

5. **Slack and AI for Team Communication**:
- o **Slack**, a popular communication platform, integrates AI-powered bots and features to help remote teams stay organized and manage their work effectively. Slackbot, for example, automates repetitive tasks like answering questions, managing reminders, and organizing channels, while AI helps filter out irrelevant information, ensuring that important messages rise to the top.
- o **Example**: **Slack's AI** uses machine learning to prioritize messages based on relevance, helping remote teams focus on the most important information and reducing the time spent on unnecessary communication.

Summary

In this chapter, we explored how **AI is enabling and supporting remote work**, becoming a critical tool for organizations and professionals to adapt to the **new**

normal of remote work. AI-powered tools enhance communication, streamline time management, automate routine tasks, and improve decision-making, ensuring that remote teams remain productive and engaged.

We also examined **tools for managing remote teams with AI**, including project management systems, performance tracking tools, and AI-based wellness platforms. These tools help managers oversee remote teams effectively, ensuring that work processes are optimized and employees remain motivated and engaged.

Through **real-world examples** like **Microsoft Teams**, **Zoom**, **Trello**, and **Slack**, we saw how AI is already playing a pivotal role in making remote work more efficient, collaborative, and manageable. As remote work continues to grow, AI will be crucial in helping organizations and workers adapt to the changing work landscape and maximize their productivity while fostering collaboration and innovation.

CHAPTER 12

AI-Powered Decision Making in Leadership Roles

The Role of AI in Strategic Decision Making

In today's fast-paced, data-driven business environment, leaders are expected to make decisions that are not only informed but also timely and accurate. **AI-powered decision-making** is becoming an essential tool for leaders, as it allows them to analyze large volumes of data, predict outcomes, and identify trends with unprecedented speed and accuracy. AI can help leaders gain deeper insights into market dynamics, customer preferences, operational efficiency, and potential risks, ultimately improving the quality and precision of strategic decisions.

1. **Data-Driven Insights for Strategic Planning**:
   - AI allows leaders to make decisions based on real-time data, historical trends, and predictive analytics. By processing vast amounts of data quickly, AI can uncover patterns that might be missed by traditional methods of analysis. This gives decision-makers the ability to make informed choices based on a comprehensive view of current and future business conditions.
   - **Example**: In **retail**, AI algorithms can analyze purchasing patterns, customer

behavior, and market trends to help executives determine which products to stock, how to price them, and where to market them for maximum impact. AI can even predict the best times to launch marketing campaigns or promotions.

2. **Predictive Analytics for Risk Management**:
   o AI-powered predictive analytics can identify potential risks before they become significant issues. For executives and managers, this means being able to foresee problems such as supply chain disruptions, financial downturns, or changing customer demands, allowing them to take proactive steps to mitigate risks.
   o **Example**: In **manufacturing**, AI models can predict machinery failures before they occur by analyzing sensor data and maintenance records. This predictive capability allows managers to schedule maintenance before costly breakdowns happen, avoiding downtime and maintaining operational efficiency.

3. **Enhancing Decision Speed and Agility**:
   o AI enables leaders to make faster decisions by automating routine tasks, gathering data, and providing actionable insights in real time. With AI, business leaders no longer have to rely on slow, manual data collection and analysis processes. AI can continuously monitor operations, customer behavior, and

market trends, helping leaders stay agile and respond quickly to changes.

- o **Example**: **Amazon's** AI-driven recommendation engine enables the company to make rapid decisions about which products to feature on its homepage based on real-time customer browsing behavior, optimizing sales and improving customer satisfaction.

4. **Scenario Simulation and Forecasting**:
   - o AI tools can simulate different scenarios and forecast potential outcomes based on various assumptions and inputs. This capability allows leaders to evaluate different strategic options and make decisions with greater confidence, knowing the likely consequences of their choices.
   - o **Example**: In **finance**, executives use AI-powered models to simulate the effects of different market conditions on the company's portfolio, helping them make informed investment decisions and protect assets in volatile markets.

AI as a Tool for Executives and Managers

Executives and managers are increasingly turning to AI as a tool to support their decision-making processes. AI systems can help leaders in multiple areas, from operational efficiency and performance monitoring to customer relationship management and financial analysis.

1. **AI for Operational Efficiency**:
   - ○ AI can assist managers in identifying inefficiencies within their operations by analyzing data and providing insights on bottlenecks, waste, and underperforming areas. AI-driven optimization tools can help managers make informed decisions to improve workflow, reduce costs, and streamline business processes.
   - ○ **Example**: In **logistics**, AI-powered route optimization tools can help managers plan delivery routes more efficiently, reducing fuel consumption, delivery times, and costs.
2. **AI for Talent Management**:
   - ○ AI can be used to enhance **human resource management** by automating recruitment, performance evaluations, and career development planning. AI tools can analyze employee data to identify high-potential candidates, provide insights into employee satisfaction, and predict retention rates.
   - ○ **Example**: AI-driven platforms like **HireVue** assist managers in the recruitment process by analyzing video interviews and ranking candidates based on their responses, helping identify the best fit for a role more quickly and accurately than traditional methods.
3. **AI for Customer and Market Insights**:
   - ○ Executives rely on AI to analyze customer feedback, social media

sentiment, and market trends to make informed decisions about product development, marketing, and sales strategies. AI systems can process large amounts of unstructured data (e.g., customer reviews, social media posts) and extract valuable insights that would be difficult for human analysts to identify.

- o **Example**: **Netflix** uses AI to analyze viewer preferences and feedback, helping executives make strategic decisions about which new shows or movies to produce, ultimately driving customer engagement and satisfaction.

4. **AI for Financial Decision-Making**:
   - o AI can assist executives in making **financial decisions** by analyzing market data, financial reports, and economic indicators. AI models can predict future market conditions, assess financial risks, and provide insights into investment opportunities, helping executives make smarter, more informed decisions.
   - o **Example**: **BlackRock**, one of the world's largest asset management firms, uses AI to manage its investment portfolio, analyzing financial data and market trends to make automated investment decisions that optimize returns while minimizing risks.

5. **AI for Real-Time Reporting and Performance Monitoring**:

- o Executives and managers can use AI to monitor key performance indicators (KPIs) in real time, allowing them to track business performance and respond quickly to changes. AI-powered dashboards provide managers with up-to-date data on sales, customer satisfaction, employee productivity, and other critical metrics.
- o **Example**: **Salesforce** uses AI to provide executives with real-time insights into customer relationships and sales team performance. Its **Einstein Analytics** tool allows managers to track sales progress, predict revenue, and optimize customer engagement strategies.

Real-World Example: AI for Financial Forecasting in Leadership

In leadership roles, **financial forecasting** is a critical function that directly influences strategic decision-making. AI is transforming how executives and financial managers forecast revenues, expenses, and profits by providing accurate predictions based on historical data and real-time market trends.

1. **AI-Powered Financial Forecasting**:
   - o AI-powered **financial forecasting tools** use machine learning algorithms to analyze historical financial data, identify patterns, and predict future financial outcomes. These tools can generate

accurate revenue projections, cash flow forecasts, and expense predictions, allowing executives to make proactive decisions about budgeting, investments, and cost management.

- o **Example**: **QuickBooks** and **Xero** use AI to help small businesses and financial managers forecast their financial future by analyzing past financial data, predicting future cash flows, and offering advice on managing expenses. These tools can also help leaders spot potential financial issues early, ensuring they can take action before problems arise.

2. **Scenario Modeling and Risk Analysis**:
   - o AI models can simulate various financial scenarios based on different assumptions, such as changes in market conditions, shifts in consumer behavior, or regulatory changes. This capability enables executives to assess the potential risks and rewards of different strategies, helping them make more informed, data-driven decisions.
   - o **Example**: In the **banking sector**, AI models are used to assess the financial impact of changing interest rates, inflation, or credit risk, enabling financial executives to make informed decisions about lending, investments, and risk management strategies.

3. **Automated Financial Reporting**:

- o AI can also automate the generation of financial reports, reducing the time and effort spent on manual data entry and analysis. These automated reports can provide real-time insights into a company's financial health, enabling executives to make decisions based on up-to-date information.
- o **Example**: **Cognizant**, a technology consulting company, uses AI to automate financial reporting, reducing the time spent on manual processes and ensuring more accurate, timely reports. These reports are used by executives to assess business performance, financial health, and investment opportunities.

4. **Predictive Analytics for Investment Decisions**:
    - o AI can analyze vast amounts of financial and market data to provide executives with insights into investment opportunities and risks. By analyzing historical performance, current market conditions, and macroeconomic trends, AI can generate recommendations for investment strategies that are more likely to yield positive returns.
    - o **Example**: **Robo-advisors** like **Betterment** and **Wealthfront** use AI to manage investment portfolios, helping executives and individual investors make informed decisions based on data-driven

insights rather than gut feeling or emotional biases.

Summary

In this chapter, we explored how **AI-powered decision-making** is becoming an indispensable tool for leaders in various sectors. We discussed the importance of AI in **strategic decision-making**, particularly its role in providing real-time insights, predictive analytics, and improved decision speed. AI enhances the decision-making process for **executives and managers** by automating routine tasks, optimizing operations, and providing critical insights into areas like **financial forecasting**, **customer behavior**, and **performance management**.

We also explored a **real-world example** of how AI is used for **financial forecasting**, demonstrating how AI tools help executives predict future financial outcomes, model different scenarios, and make smarter investment decisions. As AI continues to evolve, it will play an increasingly critical role in leadership, enabling executives to navigate complex decisions with greater accuracy, foresight, and confidence.

Leaders who embrace AI as a tool for **data-driven decision-making** will be better equipped to guide their organizations through uncertainty, optimize performance, and position their companies for future growth.

CHAPTER 13

Advanced Deep Reinforcement Learning (RL) Architectures

Understanding Advanced DQN Architectures

Deep Q-Networks (**DQN**) are a foundational architecture in **Deep Reinforcement Learning (RL)**. They combine **Q-learning**, a classic reinforcement learning algorithm, with deep neural networks to handle high-dimensional state spaces. However, as the field evolved, several improvements and advanced architectures were proposed to solve some of the issues in standard DQN. These architectures aim to make reinforcement learning more efficient, stable, and capable of tackling more complex problems.

The basic **DQN** algorithm involves learning the optimal action-value function, **Q(s, a)**, using a deep neural network to approximate it. However, as with any deep learning model, **overestimation bias** and inefficiencies in training can cause the model to perform suboptimally in certain tasks. Over the years, several advanced techniques and architectures have been introduced to overcome these challenges, leading to more stable and efficient learning in RL.

Double DQN and How It Solves the Overestimation Bias

One of the main challenges with standard DQN is **overestimation bias**. In Q-learning, the action-value

125

function is updated using the **max operator**, which selects the maximum predicted Q-value for the next state. This can lead to overestimation, especially when the network is poorly trained or the Q-values are inaccurate.

Double DQN (DDQN) is an improvement over standard DQN that specifically addresses the overestimation bias by using two separate networks for action selection and evaluation. The idea is to decouple the selection of the action from the evaluation of the Q-value, which reduces the risk of overestimation.

1. **How Double DQN Works**:
   - In **Double DQN**, the action selection and the Q-value evaluation are handled by two different networks:
     - **Main Q-Network**: Selects the action to take in the next state.
     - **Target Q-Network**: Evaluates the Q-value of the selected action.
   - This helps in reducing the overestimation bias because the same Q-network is not responsible for both selecting the action and evaluating it.
2. **Mathematical Representation**:
   - The update rule in Double DQN becomes: $y = r + \gamma Q'(s', \text{argmax}_a Q(s', a; \theta); \theta^-)$ where $Q(s', a; \theta)$ is the Q-value predicted by the main Q-network,

and $Q'(s', a; \theta^-)$ is the Q-value predicted by the target Q-network.

3. **Benefits of Double DQN**:
   - Double DQN reduces the bias introduced by using the max operator in standard DQN, leading to more stable training and more accurate Q-value estimates.

Dueling DQN, Prioritized Experience Replay, and A3C

In addition to Double DQN, several other advanced techniques have been proposed to enhance the efficiency and stability of Deep RL algorithms:

1. **Dueling DQN**:
   - The **Dueling DQN** architecture introduces two separate estimators for the Q-value: one for the **state-value** function and another for the **advantage** function. This allows the network to better separate the value of a state from the relative advantage of taking a specific action in that state.
   - The Q-value is then represented as: $Q(s,a)=V(s)+A(s,a)$ $Q(s, a) = V(s) + A(s, a)$ $Q(s,a)=V(s)+A(s,a)$ where:
     - **V(s)** is the value of the state.
     - **A(s, a)** is the advantage of taking action **a** in state **s**.
   - **Benefits**: This helps the network focus on learning useful state representations, especially in environments where the

value of states is more important than the relative advantage of specific actions.

2. **Prioritized Experience Replay (PER)**:

   o **Experience Replay** is a technique where past experiences (state, action, reward, next state) are stored in a replay buffer and sampled randomly for training. However, this approach doesn't prioritize experiences that are more important or informative for learning.

   o **Prioritized Experience Replay (PER)** modifies this approach by prioritizing experiences based on their **TD-error** (temporal difference error), which measures how surprising or valuable a given experience is for the model's learning.

   o **Benefits**: By prioritizing experiences that have a higher learning potential, PER accelerates the training process and helps the agent learn faster and more efficiently.

3. **Asynchronous Advantage Actor-Critic (A3C)**:

   o The **A3C** algorithm is another significant improvement in Deep RL. It is an **actor-critic** method, where the **actor** selects actions based on a policy and the **critic** evaluates the action using the value function. What sets A3C apart is its **asynchronous** nature: multiple agents are trained in parallel, each with their own copy of the environment and model.

   o **Key Features**:

- **Multiple workers**: A3C uses multiple agents that explore the environment in parallel, helping to improve data diversity and reduce the correlation between experiences.
- **Advantage Function**: The **advantage function** estimates how much better an action is compared to the average action, stabilizing learning by reducing the variance of the policy gradient.
  - **Benefits**: The asynchronous nature of A3C reduces the variance in updates, improves the stability of training, and accelerates the learning process.

Hands-On Example: Implementing Advanced RL Algorithms in Python

Let's implement a simplified version of the **Double DQN** algorithm in Python using **PyTorch**. We'll use the **OpenAI Gym** environment to demonstrate how Double DQN can be implemented for an RL problem.

```python
python
Copy
import torch
import torch.nn as nn
import torch.optim as optim
import random
import numpy as np
from collections import deque
```

```python
import gym

# Hyperparameters
learning_rate = 0.001
gamma = 0.99
epsilon = 0.1
batch_size = 64
buffer_size = 10000
target_update_frequency = 10

# Define the Q-network architecture
class QNetwork(nn.Module):
    def __init__(self, state_size,
action_size):
        super(QNetwork,
self).__init__()
        self.fc1                      =
nn.Linear(state_size, 128)
        self.fc2    =    nn.Linear(128,
128)
        self.fc3    =    nn.Linear(128,
action_size)

    def forward(self, state):
        x                             =
torch.relu(self.fc1(state))
        x = torch.relu(self.fc2(x))
        return self.fc3(x)

# Double DQN Agent
class DoubleDQNAgent:
    def __init__(self, state_size,
action_size):
```

```python
        self.action_size         =
action_size
        self.state_size = state_size
        self.memory               =
deque(maxlen=buffer_size)
        self.main_model           =
QNetwork(state_size,
action_size).to(device)
        self.target_model         =
QNetwork(state_size,
action_size).to(device)
        self.optimizer            =
optim.Adam(self.main_model.parameter
s(), lr=learning_rate)
        self.update_target_model()

    def update_target_model(self):

self.target_model.load_state_dict(se
lf.main_model.state_dict())

    def act(self, state):
        if random.random() < epsilon:
            return
random.choice(range(self.action_size
))  # Random action (exploration)
        state                     =
torch.FloatTensor(state).unsqueeze(0
).to(device)
        q_values                  =
self.main_model(state)
        return
torch.argmax(q_values).item()        #
```

Select the action with the highest Q-value

```
    def store(self, state, action,
reward, next_state, done):
        self.memory.append((state,
action, reward, next_state, done))

    def learn(self):
        if    len(self.memory)    <
batch_size:
            return

        batch                    =
random.sample(self.memory,
batch_size)
        states,   actions,   rewards,
next_states, dones = zip(*batch)

        states                    =
torch.FloatTensor(states).to(device)
        next_states               =
torch.FloatTensor(next_states).to(de
vice)
        rewards                   =
torch.FloatTensor(rewards).to(device
)
        dones                     =
torch.FloatTensor(dones).to(device)

        # Get Q-values for current
states and actions
```

```
        q_values                  =
self.main_model(states).gather(1,
torch.LongTensor(actions).unsqueeze(
1).to(device))

        # Get next state Q-values from
target network
        next_q_values              =
self.target_model(next_states).max(1
)[0].unsqueeze(1)

        # Compute the target Q-values
        target_q_values = rewards +
(gamma * next_q_values * (1 - dones))

        # Compute loss and optimize
        loss = nn.MSELoss()(q_values,
target_q_values)
        self.optimizer.zero_grad()
        loss.backward()
        self.optimizer.step()

# Training loop
env = gym.make('CartPole-v1')
agent                             =
DoubleDQNAgent(state_size=env.observ
ation_space.shape[0],
action_size=env.action_space.n)
episodes = 1000
device   =   torch.device("cuda"   if
torch.cuda.is_available() else "cpu")

for e in range(episodes):
```

```
state = env.reset()
total_reward = 0
done = False

while not done:
    action = agent.act(state)
    next_state, reward, done, _ =
env.step(action)
    agent.store(state,      action,
reward, next_state, done)
    agent.learn()
    total_reward += reward
    state = next_state

if e % target_update_frequency ==
0:
    agent.update_target_model()

print(f"Episode     {e+1},     Total
Reward: {total_reward}")
```

Summary

In this chapter, we delved into **advanced Deep Q-Network (DQN) architectures**, including **Double DQN, Dueling DQN, Prioritized Experience Replay**, and **Asynchronous Advantage Actor-Critic (A3C)**. These advanced algorithms address several limitations in standard DQN, such as **overestimation bias**, **instability**, and **inefficient exploration**.

We also explored how these architectures contribute to making **Deep RL** more efficient and stable by enhancing performance and allowing agents to learn from more meaningful experiences. Through a **hands-on example**, we demonstrated how to implement a **Double DQN** algorithm using **PyTorch** in an RL task with the **OpenAI Gym** environment.

These techniques are widely used in more complex environments and problems, including robotics, gaming, and financial forecasting, where learning from large datasets and continuous interaction with dynamic environments is critical.

CHAPTER 14

AI in Marketing: A New Era of Customer Interaction

AI's Role in Personalized Marketing Strategies

In recent years, **AI** has revolutionized the way businesses approach **marketing**. One of the most significant shifts has been the movement toward **personalized marketing**, where AI technologies help businesses tailor their strategies to individual customer preferences, behaviors, and interactions. Personalization at scale has become a powerful tool for improving customer engagement, satisfaction, and ultimately, sales.

1. **Customer Segmentation**:
   - **AI-powered algorithms** can analyze vast amounts of customer data (from browsing behavior to purchase history) to segment customers into highly specific groups. This segmentation allows businesses to create highly targeted marketing campaigns that are more likely to resonate with the audience.
   - **Example**: Retailers like **Amazon** and **Netflix** use AI to segment their customer base by analyzing past purchases, watch history, and other data. This enables them to recommend products or content that are highly relevant to individual users,

making their marketing efforts more efficient and effective.

2. **Predictive Analytics**:
   - Predictive analytics, powered by AI, is another critical tool for personalized marketing. By analyzing past behaviors and trends, AI can forecast future customer actions, such as which products they are likely to buy, when they might make a purchase, or even when they are likely to churn.
   - **Example**: In **email marketing**, AI can help predict the best time to send emails to customers based on their past interactions, leading to higher open and click-through rates. For instance, an e-commerce company might use AI to predict which customers are likely to abandon their shopping carts and send targeted emails to encourage them to complete their purchase.

3. **Dynamic Pricing**:
   - AI can help companies implement **dynamic pricing** strategies, where prices are adjusted in real-time based on customer behavior, market demand, competitor pricing, and other external factors. This is particularly useful in industries like **travel**, **e-commerce**, and **event ticketing**, where demand can fluctuate dramatically.
   - **Example**: **Airlines** use AI algorithms to adjust flight prices based on demand,

customer searches, and competitor pricing, ensuring that they remain competitive and maximize revenue.

4. **Enhanced Customer Experience**:
    o AI plays a crucial role in improving the overall customer experience by providing personalized recommendations, relevant content, and even customer support. Personalized experiences increase customer loyalty, improve engagement, and encourage repeat business.
    o **Example**: In the **fashion industry**, AI tools like **Stitch Fix** use customer data, including style preferences, body type, and previous purchases, to recommend clothing items that are tailored to each customer's taste, enhancing the shopping experience and increasing sales.

Chatbots, Predictive Analytics, and AI-Driven Content Creation

AI has also enhanced several key areas of marketing, such as **customer support**, **content creation**, and **predictive analytics**. These advancements allow businesses to engage with customers more effectively and provide relevant, timely information.

1. **Chatbots and Virtual Assistants**:
    o **AI-powered chatbots** are now a standard tool for businesses, particularly in customer service and lead generation. These bots can interact with customers in

real-time, answer questions, guide them through processes, and even resolve issues. By using **natural language processing (NLP)**, chatbots can understand and respond to a wide range of customer inquiries, improving the customer experience and freeing up human agents for more complex tasks.

- o **Example**: **Sephora** uses a chatbot called **Sephora Virtual Artist** to guide customers through their product selections. The chatbot uses AI to provide personalized product recommendations based on customers' beauty preferences and needs, improving the shopping experience.

2. **Predictive Analytics for Campaign Effectiveness**:
   - o Predictive analytics powered by AI can optimize marketing campaigns by analyzing historical data and predicting future trends. Marketers can use AI to forecast customer behavior, identify the most effective channels for engagement, and determine the ideal time and format for campaigns.
   - o **Example**: **Coca-Cola** uses AI-driven analytics to predict consumer behavior and optimize its marketing campaigns. By analyzing social media activity, purchase data, and even weather patterns, Coca-Cola tailors its advertisements to resonate with customers at the right time and place.

3. **AI-Driven Content Creation**:
   - o AI is also making waves in content creation by automating tasks such as copywriting, video generation, and social media management. With the help of **natural language generation (NLG)** tools, AI can generate human-like text for blog posts, product descriptions, and even email marketing campaigns, ensuring that content is both relevant and engaging.
   - o **Example**: **Wordsmith**, an AI-powered content creation platform, uses NLG to generate personalized reports, blog posts, and product descriptions. Brands use Wordsmith to create large volumes of content efficiently, ensuring consistent messaging across channels without sacrificing quality.
4. **AI for Visual Content Creation**:
   - o In addition to text, AI is also revolutionizing the creation of **visual content**, such as images, graphics, and videos. **Generative Adversarial Networks (GANs)** and other AI tools can be used to automatically generate images and video content based on specific parameters, saving time and effort for marketers while enabling more personalized visuals.
   - o **Example**: **L'Oreal** uses AI to create personalized beauty ads, allowing customers to see themselves in makeup advertisements through augmented reality

(AR) technology. This use of AI helps create more personalized and engaging content for consumers, enhancing brand loyalty and engagement.

Real-World Example: AI-Powered Advertising in E-Commerce

E-commerce businesses have been among the first to adopt AI-powered marketing tools to improve customer engagement, boost sales, and optimize advertising efforts. AI allows e-commerce companies to create highly personalized shopping experiences, from targeted advertising to dynamic pricing and product recommendations.

1. **Personalized Recommendations**:
    o AI-driven recommendation engines are now a standard feature on most e-commerce platforms. These systems analyze a user's browsing history, previous purchases, and other behavioral data to suggest products that are most likely to appeal to them.
    o **Example**: **Amazon's** recommendation engine is powered by machine learning algorithms that analyze user behavior and provide personalized product suggestions. This system contributes significantly to Amazon's sales by driving **cross-selling** and **upselling** opportunities, ensuring that customers are presented

with relevant products they are most likely to purchase.

2. **Targeted Advertising**:
   o AI enables **hyper-targeted advertising**, where e-commerce companies can serve personalized ads to users based on their online behavior, demographics, and preferences. This allows advertisers to reach their most valuable audience with minimal wasted spend.
   o **Example: Facebook Ads** uses AI to help advertisers target potential customers by analyzing users' browsing habits, interests, and interactions with previous ads. This AI-powered system allows e-commerce companies to show highly relevant ads to individual users, improving conversion rates and ad performance.

3. **Dynamic Pricing**:
   o AI allows e-commerce businesses to implement **dynamic pricing strategies**, where the price of a product can fluctuate based on factors such as demand, competition, and customer behavior. This helps businesses remain competitive while maximizing revenue.
   o **Example: Airbnb** uses AI to adjust pricing dynamically based on factors like **demand, seasonality**, and **competition** from other listings. By offering competitive and tailored pricing, Airbnb

can increase bookings and optimize host revenue.

4. **AI in Retargeting Campaigns**:

   o **Retargeting** is a powerful marketing tactic that uses AI to serve ads to users who have previously interacted with a website or app but did not complete a purchase. By analyzing browsing history and behavior, AI can ensure that the right ads are shown to the right people, increasing the likelihood of conversion.

   o **Example**: **Shopify** uses AI to help e-commerce businesses run successful retargeting campaigns, serving personalized ads to users who abandoned their shopping carts. This use of AI has proven effective in recovering lost sales and improving customer retention.

Summary

In this chapter, we explored how **AI is revolutionizing marketing**, particularly through **personalized marketing strategies, chatbots, predictive analytics**, and **AI-driven content creation**. AI enables businesses to deliver tailored, relevant experiences to customers, improving engagement, conversion rates, and customer satisfaction. By leveraging AI for **customer segmentation, dynamic pricing, personalized recommendations**, and more, businesses can enhance their marketing efforts and create a more personalized, efficient, and effective approach.

We also examined real-world examples, particularly in **e-commerce**, where AI is transforming the way companies interact with their customers. **Amazon's** recommendation engine, **Facebook Ads**, **Airbnb's dynamic pricing**, and **Shopify's retargeting campaigns** demonstrate the power of AI in creating more efficient, personalized, and impactful marketing strategies.

As AI continues to evolve, its role in marketing will only grow, offering even more opportunities for businesses to connect with their customers, optimize their campaigns, and drive business success in a competitive landscape.

CHAPTER 15

The Role of AI in Innovation and Product Development

AI's Role in Accelerating Innovation

Artificial Intelligence (AI) is a driving force in **innovation**, enabling businesses to push the boundaries of what's possible in product development, service delivery, and process optimization. AI accelerates the speed at which new ideas are generated, tested, and brought to market, significantly reducing the time and costs traditionally associated with innovation cycles.

1. **Automating Idea Generation**:
   - o AI can help businesses generate ideas for new products or features by analyzing large volumes of data from various sources such as customer feedback, market trends, social media conversations, and competitor products. Machine learning models can identify gaps in the market, unmet customer needs, and emerging trends, offering businesses valuable insights for product innovation.
   - o **Example**: Companies in the **fashion industry**, like **Stitch Fix**, use AI to analyze fashion trends and customer preferences, helping designers create new collections based on data-driven insights.

AI assists in predicting which styles, colors, and fabrics will be popular in upcoming seasons, driving faster innovation cycles in product development.

2. **Predicting Market Demand**:
    o One of AI's major strengths in innovation is its ability to predict **market demand** for new products. By analyzing historical sales data, customer behavior, and market conditions, AI can forecast which product features, designs, or services are likely to succeed and when the market is ready for them. This helps companies reduce the risk of launching products that may not resonate with consumers.
    o **Example**: **Apple** uses AI and data analysis to forecast customer demand for specific features in new iPhone models, such as screen size, camera capabilities, or battery life. By understanding customer preferences, Apple can make data-driven decisions about which features to prioritize, ensuring that new products align with market demand.

3. **Enhancing Creative Collaboration**:
    o AI-powered tools enhance collaboration among teams involved in the **innovation** process. By automating routine tasks, AI enables employees to focus more on creativity and problem-solving, which are essential for innovation. AI systems can also provide feedback and suggestions,

creating a more dynamic and efficient creative process.

- o **Example**: In the **film industry**, AI is being used to help screenwriters and filmmakers generate new ideas for scripts or storylines. Tools like **Plotagon** use AI to analyze existing movies, books, and user preferences to suggest creative directions and themes for new content.

4. **Speeding Up Research and Development (R&D)**:
   - o AI is accelerating **research and development** by enabling faster data analysis, modeling, and simulation. In industries like pharmaceuticals and biotechnology, AI is used to quickly analyze vast amounts of data and identify new opportunities for product development, significantly reducing the time and cost involved in R&D.
   - o **Example: Insilico Medicine** uses AI to analyze biological data and discover new drug compounds. The company uses machine learning models to predict how new drugs will interact with specific diseases, speeding up the R&D process and reducing the need for lengthy clinical trials.

How AI is Used in Product Design and Prototyping

AI is not only helping businesses accelerate innovation in idea generation and market forecasting, but it is also transforming the **product design** and **prototyping** phases of product development. AI tools and algorithms can automate repetitive design tasks, simulate prototypes, and provide insights into design efficiency, helping designers create better products in less time.

1. **AI-Driven Design Tools**:
    o   AI-powered **design software** allows designers to automate many of the tasks involved in creating products, from sketching initial concepts to optimizing shapes and sizes for functionality. AI can help designers explore more design options by rapidly generating variations and comparing them to find the best possible solution.
    o   **Example: Autodesk Fusion 360** is an AI-driven design tool used by engineers and product designers. The software uses machine learning to suggest design optimizations and simulate how different materials and designs will perform under real-world conditions, making it easier to create functional prototypes.

2. **Generative Design**:
    o   **Generative design** is a process where AI algorithms create multiple design alternatives based on predefined constraints and goals, such as weight, strength, and material usage. By using AI to explore countless design variations, businesses can uncover innovative solutions that would be difficult or

impossible for humans to design manually.

- o **Example**: **Airbus** uses generative design powered by AI to create lightweight and efficient aircraft parts. The AI algorithm takes into account various factors, such as material properties and aerodynamic performance, and generates design options that meet the specifications while minimizing weight and material usage.

3. **Prototyping with AI Simulation**:
   - o AI can speed up the **prototyping** phase by simulating how a product will perform in real-world conditions. This reduces the need for physical prototypes, allowing companies to test and refine designs faster and at a lower cost. AI-powered simulations can predict how a product will behave under different conditions, such as stress, temperature, and usage.
   - o **Example**: **Nike** uses AI-powered simulations to test the performance of its new **running shoes**. The simulation takes into account factors like foot movement, pressure, and material flexing, allowing Nike to refine their designs without needing to build multiple physical prototypes.

4. **3D Printing and AI Integration**:
   - o AI is also integrated with **3D printing** technologies to optimize the creation of prototypes. AI-driven 3D printers can adjust parameters in real time to improve

design accuracy, material usage, and production speed. This integration is particularly useful in industries like automotive, aerospace, and consumer electronics, where rapid prototyping is critical.

- o **Example**: **Ford** uses AI and 3D printing to create automotive prototypes. The AI system monitors the 3D printing process, ensuring that each layer is printed accurately, reducing errors and material waste during prototype creation.

Real-World Example: AI in Tech Product Development (e.g., Smartphones)

The tech industry, particularly smartphone manufacturers, has been at the forefront of adopting AI to drive innovation and product development. AI plays a pivotal role in various stages of smartphone design, from conceptualization and prototyping to production and marketing. In this section, we will explore how AI has been leveraged in smartphone development to create groundbreaking devices and enhance user experience.

1. **AI in Smartphone Hardware Design**:
   - o AI is used in the hardware design phase of smartphones to improve components such as processors, cameras, and battery life. By simulating different design parameters and using generative design techniques, AI helps create more efficient and

powerful hardware while minimizing the size and weight of the device.

- o **Example**: **Apple**'s **A-series chips**, used in iPhones, are designed using AI algorithms that optimize the chip's performance and power efficiency. These AI-powered chips process data faster while consuming less energy, enhancing both the speed and battery life of the device.

2. **AI in Smartphone Software and User Experience**:
    - o AI is integral to enhancing the software and **user experience** (UX) of smartphones. AI-powered features like **face recognition**, **voice assistants**, **camera enhancements**, and **personalized recommendations** have become standard in modern smartphones.
    - o **Example**: **Google**'s **Pixel phones** use AI for features like **Night Sight**, which enhances low-light photography, and **Call Screen**, an AI-powered feature that helps users avoid spam calls by automatically screening and blocking unwanted callers. These AI-driven features improve the overall user experience and differentiate the device in a competitive market.

3. **AI in Smartphone Camera Systems**:
    - o The smartphone **camera** has evolved significantly with the help of AI. AI algorithms help optimize images in real-time, adjust settings like exposure and

white balance, and even create artistic effects like portrait mode. Additionally, AI-powered cameras can recognize objects and scenes, automatically adjusting settings to produce the best shot.

- o **Example**: **Huawei**'s **P30 Pro** uses AI to enhance camera performance. AI algorithms analyze scenes, detect subjects like faces, landscapes, or food, and adjust settings accordingly to produce professional-quality photos, even for amateur photographers.

4. **AI in Smartphone Manufacturing**:
   - o AI plays a crucial role in optimizing the **manufacturing** process of smartphones. By automating tasks such as quality control, assembly, and defect detection, AI helps manufacturers improve production efficiency and reduce errors.
   - o **Example**: **Samsung** uses AI to streamline the assembly process of its smartphones. AI-powered robots are used in the production line to test components, such as screens and cameras, for defects, ensuring that only high-quality units reach customers.

Summary

In this chapter, we explored how **AI accelerates innovation** and drives product development by automating tasks, generating ideas, and optimizing designs. AI's role in personalized marketing strategies, rapid prototyping, and design has significantly changed how products are brought to market. Through **generative design**, **predictive analytics**, and **AI-powered simulations**, businesses can now develop products faster, with higher quality and greater efficiency.

We also highlighted **real-world examples** of AI in **tech product development**, specifically in **smartphones**. AI has enhanced everything from hardware design and camera technology to software optimization and manufacturing processes. Through the integration of AI, companies like **Apple**, **Huawei**, and **Google** have been able to push the boundaries of innovation, creating products that are more powerful, efficient, and user-friendly.

As AI continues to evolve, its role in **innovation and product development** will only increase, enabling businesses to respond more quickly to market demands, optimize their operations, and deliver more personalized products and experiences.

CHAPTER 16

AI and Cybersecurity: Protecting the Workforce

How AI is Used in Cybersecurity

Cybersecurity has become an essential part of modern business operations as organizations face increasingly sophisticated cyber threats. Traditional security measures, like firewalls and antivirus software, are no longer sufficient to protect against advanced threats. This is where **Artificial Intelligence (AI)** has become a game-changer in the field of cybersecurity. AI systems are capable of analyzing vast amounts of data, identifying patterns, and responding to threats in real-time—making them indispensable for proactive cybersecurity strategies.

1. **AI for Threat Detection**:
    o AI can help identify potential security threats by analyzing network traffic, user behavior, and system activities for unusual patterns or anomalies. Machine learning algorithms, particularly **unsupervised learning**, are effective at identifying zero-day threats and sophisticated attack vectors that may not be detected by traditional methods.
    o **Example**: **Darktrace**, a cybersecurity company, uses AI to detect **anomalous activity** in real-time by modeling the

"normal" behavior of a network. Once the AI system learns what constitutes regular activity, it can flag any deviations—such as unusual login attempts, data exfiltration, or unauthorized access—allowing security teams to respond proactively.

2. **AI for Automating Incident Response**:
   o AI can automate many aspects of incident response, helping organizations reduce the time it takes to detect, assess, and mitigate cybersecurity threats. AI systems can automatically trigger responses such as isolating affected systems, blocking malicious IP addresses, or applying patches to vulnerabilities without requiring human intervention.
   o **Example**: **Cortex XSOAR** (formerly Demisto) by Palo Alto Networks is an AI-powered Security Orchestration, Automation, and Response (SOAR) platform that automates routine cybersecurity tasks such as data collection, analysis, and response. This allows security teams to focus on more complex threats while ensuring that basic tasks are handled promptly.

3. **AI for Malware Detection**:
   o AI and machine learning techniques, such as **deep learning** and **neural networks**, can help detect new forms of malware by recognizing patterns in files or behavior rather than relying on known signatures.

These AI systems can identify previously unknown malware, including polymorphic or metamorphic malware that changes its form to avoid detection.

- o **Example**: **CrowdStrike** uses AI to detect **malicious behavior** and file patterns associated with malware. Their system identifies new malware strains by learning from large datasets of known threats and then applying this knowledge to new, unseen malware attempts.

4. **AI for Phishing Detection**:
   - o Phishing attacks, where cybercriminals attempt to trick individuals into revealing sensitive information, are one of the most common cybersecurity threats. AI-powered systems can scan emails, websites, and messages to detect suspicious content, such as fake URLs, domain impersonations, and unusual language patterns, helping to protect employees from falling victim to these attacks.
   - o **Example**: **Barracuda Networks** uses AI to identify phishing emails by analyzing the content of the email and comparing it to known phishing tactics. The system can flag suspicious emails and automatically quarantine them before they reach the user's inbox.

5. **AI in Behavioral Analytics**:
   - o **User and Entity Behavior Analytics (UEBA)** powered by AI helps identify

threats by analyzing the normal behavior of users and entities (devices, applications, etc.) within an organization. By establishing a baseline of normal activity, AI can quickly detect deviations that may indicate a compromised user account or insider threat.

- o **Example**: **Vectra AI** uses UEBA to monitor network traffic and detect potential threats by identifying abnormal user behaviors. Their AI system can automatically classify attacks such as insider threats, credential theft, and data exfiltration, helping organizations respond to threats before they escalate.

The Challenges of Securing AI Systems and Data

While AI brings numerous benefits to cybersecurity, it also introduces several challenges, particularly when it comes to securing **AI systems** and the data they rely on. As AI is increasingly used to defend against cyber threats, cybercriminals are also leveraging AI to launch attacks, making it essential to secure both the systems and the data that AI systems use and generate.

1. **Adversarial Attacks on AI Systems**:
   - o One of the significant challenges in securing AI systems is the risk of **adversarial attacks**, where attackers manipulate the input data in subtle ways to deceive AI models. In the context of cybersecurity, adversarial attacks can

target AI-based threat detection systems, causing them to misclassify benign behavior as malicious or vice versa.

- o **Example**: In AI-driven security systems, attackers could craft **adversarial inputs** (e.g., malicious traffic disguised as legitimate) that confuse the AI into allowing the attack to pass undetected. This highlights the need for AI systems to be robust and resilient to such attacks.

2. **Data Privacy and Integrity**:
   - o AI systems rely heavily on large datasets to learn and make decisions. Ensuring the **privacy** and **integrity** of this data is critical, as compromised data can lead to erroneous conclusions and expose sensitive information. AI systems that process sensitive data must comply with data protection regulations (e.g., **GDPR**) to prevent unauthorized access and maintain the confidentiality of personal information.
   - o **Example**: If an AI model used for cybersecurity is trained on sensitive data from a company's employees, ensuring that this data is securely stored and processed is vital. If this data is compromised, attackers could gain insight into internal systems and use it for future attacks.

3. **Securing AI Models from Theft or Manipulation**:

- AI models themselves can become targets of attacks. **Model theft** occurs when an attacker gains unauthorized access to an AI model, allowing them to reverse-engineer it and exploit it for malicious purposes. Furthermore, AI models can be manipulated to misbehave, known as **model poisoning**, which can undermine the security of AI-driven systems.
- **Example**: A **machine learning model** used in threat detection could be poisoned by feeding it malicious training data, causing the model to perform poorly and miss important threats. Securing the model from tampering is essential to maintaining the integrity of the system.

4. **Bias and Fairness in AI**:
   - AI systems are only as good as the data they are trained on. If the data used to train a cybersecurity AI model is biased or incomplete, the system may fail to detect certain types of attacks or identify malicious behavior in certain contexts. Ensuring that AI models are trained on diverse, representative, and balanced data is crucial for reducing bias and improving security.
   - **Example**: If a cybersecurity AI model is trained on data from a specific geographical region or industry, it may not be effective at detecting cyber threats from other regions or industries that have different attack vectors or behaviors.

Real-World Example: AI-Driven Threat Detection Systems

AI-powered **threat detection systems** are among the most widely used AI applications in cybersecurity. These systems leverage machine learning, behavioral analytics, and deep learning to identify and respond to security threats in real-time. These systems are capable of detecting a wide range of attacks, from malware and phishing to insider threats and DDoS (Distributed Denial of Service) attacks.

1. **Darktrace**:
   - **Darktrace** uses **AI-powered cybersecurity** systems that learn the "normal" patterns of activity within an organization's network. The system uses machine learning to detect any deviations from these patterns that could indicate a potential security breach, such as malware, ransomware, or phishing attempts.
   - **Example**: Darktrace's **Enterprise Immune System** continuously monitors network traffic and can detect novel and previously unseen cyber threats by identifying anomalies in behavior. The system learns from data over time, improving its accuracy and reducing false positives. In a real-world scenario, Darktrace detected a **ransomware attack** before it could spread across the network, preventing a major breach.

2. **CrowdStrike**:
    o   **CrowdStrike** is a leading provider of AI-driven endpoint protection and threat detection. Their **Falcon platform** uses machine learning and AI to analyze endpoint activity and detect suspicious behavior in real time. The system provides proactive defense against cyberattacks by continuously monitoring the activities of all devices connected to a network.
    o   **Example**: **CrowdStrike Falcon** identified an advanced **phishing campaign** targeting financial institutions, using AI-powered threat intelligence to block the attack before any data was compromised. Falcon also uses predictive analytics to identify potential attack vectors, enabling businesses to take preventive action.
3. **IBM Watson for Cyber Security**:
    o   **IBM Watson** leverages AI to assist cybersecurity teams in identifying, investigating, and responding to security threats. It analyzes vast amounts of data from various sources, such as security logs, threat intelligence feeds, and incident reports, to provide security professionals with actionable insights.
    o   **Example**: **IBM Watson for Cyber Security** is used by companies like **SoftBank** to improve threat detection capabilities. Watson helps organizations

understand security data by analyzing it with natural language processing and machine learning algorithms, identifying emerging threats that might be missed by traditional systems.

Summary

In this chapter, we discussed the growing role of **AI in cybersecurity**, focusing on its ability to detect threats, automate incident responses, and improve the overall security posture of organizations. AI-powered systems such as **Darktrace**, **CrowdStrike**, and **IBM Watson** have significantly enhanced threat detection and prevention by using machine learning, behavioral analytics, and predictive models.

We also explored the **challenges of securing AI systems** and the data they rely on. From **adversarial attacks** on AI models to ensuring **data privacy** and **model integrity**, securing AI-driven systems is essential to maintaining the overall security of an organization. As cyber threats continue to evolve, AI will play an increasingly critical role in detecting and mitigating risks before they cause significant harm.

As businesses continue to integrate AI into their cybersecurity strategies, it is crucial to ensure that both AI systems and the data they rely on are secure, transparent, and resilient to malicious attacks. AI's potential to protect the workforce from cyber threats is vast, but it requires a thoughtful, proactive approach to ensure its effectiveness and safeguard the integrity of the systems it is designed to protect.

CHAPTER 17

The Future of AI in Healthcare: Opportunities and Challenges

How AI is Revolutionizing the Healthcare Industry

The healthcare industry is undergoing a massive transformation, and at the heart of this revolution is **Artificial Intelligence (AI)**. AI is increasingly being used to optimize healthcare services, improve patient outcomes, and reduce operational costs. By analyzing vast amounts of medical data, automating tasks, and predicting patient needs, AI is playing a crucial role in reshaping the future of healthcare.

1. **Improved Decision-Making**:
    o AI is helping healthcare professionals make more informed and accurate decisions. Through advanced machine learning models and deep learning algorithms, AI can analyze complex medical data—such as medical images, patient records, and genetic information—much faster and more accurately than humans. This can lead to better diagnosis and treatment decisions.
    o **Example**: AI systems, like **IBM Watson for Health**, can analyze a patient's medical history, genetic data, and clinical studies to recommend personalized

treatment options, assisting doctors in choosing the most effective therapies.

2. **Streamlining Administrative Tasks**:
   - AI is also being used to automate administrative functions in healthcare, such as scheduling, billing, and patient documentation. These repetitive tasks are time-consuming and prone to error when done manually. AI can streamline these processes, reducing the burden on healthcare professionals and allowing them to focus more on patient care.
   - **Example**: AI-powered chatbots can help answer patient queries, schedule appointments, and even manage insurance claims, improving the overall efficiency of healthcare systems and reducing administrative overhead.

3. **Enhancing Access to Healthcare**:
   - AI has the potential to bridge the gap in healthcare access, especially in remote or underserved regions. With AI-driven telemedicine, patients can access healthcare services from the comfort of their homes, regardless of their geographical location.
   - **Example**: AI-based telehealth platforms, such as **Babylon Health**, provide virtual consultations with doctors, AI-driven symptom checkers, and even diagnostic tools that can analyze medical conditions, making healthcare more accessible to people around the world.

4. **Reducing Healthcare Costs**:
   - ○ AI can help reduce the costs of healthcare by improving efficiency, preventing unnecessary procedures, and optimizing resource allocation. For example, AI models can predict which patients are at risk of developing certain conditions, allowing for early intervention and preventive care, which can ultimately save money for both patients and healthcare providers.
   - ○ **Example**: AI-powered systems in **hospitals** can predict patient admissions and discharges, optimize bed occupancy, and even help schedule surgeries, ensuring that resources are used efficiently, reducing waste, and lowering costs.

AI Applications in Diagnostics, Treatment, and Patient Care

AI has shown great promise in enhancing various aspects of healthcare, including **diagnostics**, **treatment planning**, and **patient care**. By leveraging machine learning and other AI technologies, healthcare providers are improving the accuracy and timeliness of diagnoses, personalizing treatment plans, and offering more efficient care to patients.

1. **AI in Diagnostics**:
   - ○ AI is transforming medical diagnostics by enabling faster and more accurate

detection of diseases. Machine learning models are capable of analyzing medical images (e.g., CT scans, MRIs, X-rays) to identify anomalies and detect conditions such as cancer, heart disease, and neurological disorders at earlier stages when they are most treatable.

- o **Example**: **Google Health**'s AI-powered deep learning model for breast cancer detection outperformed radiologists in some cases, detecting tumors with a higher accuracy and lower false-positive rate. This AI tool assists radiologists in diagnosing cancer, providing them with a second opinion and improving diagnostic accuracy.

2. **AI in Personalized Treatment**:
   - o **Personalized medicine** aims to tailor medical treatments to individual patients based on their unique genetic makeup, lifestyle, and other factors. AI plays a key role in personalized treatment by analyzing large sets of patient data and suggesting customized treatment plans.
   - o **Example**: **Tempus**, a technology company focused on personalized cancer care, uses AI to analyze clinical and molecular data to recommend targeted therapies. By using AI to compare a patient's genomic data with a vast database of treatment outcomes, doctors can select the most effective treatment plans for individual cancer patients.

3. **AI in Drug Discovery**:
   - AI is being used to accelerate the **drug discovery process** by analyzing vast amounts of chemical, biological, and clinical data. AI can predict how different compounds will interact with the body, identify potential drug candidates, and even help design new drugs more efficiently.
   - **Example**: **Insilico Medicine**, an AI-driven drug discovery company, uses machine learning algorithms to analyze biological data and discover new drugs. Their AI platform has been successful in identifying potential drug candidates for diseases such as cancer and fibrosis, reducing the time and cost associated with drug development.

4. **AI in Monitoring and Patient Care**:
   - AI is also being used to monitor patients in real time and improve care by continuously assessing their condition. Wearable devices equipped with AI algorithms can monitor vital signs like heart rate, blood pressure, and oxygen levels, sending alerts to healthcare providers if any abnormal patterns are detected.
   - **Example**: **Fitbit** and **Apple Watch** offer health-monitoring features, including heart rate tracking and ECGs. These devices use AI algorithms to detect irregularities in heart rhythms and alert

the user or a healthcare provider, potentially preventing heart attacks or strokes.

Real-World Example: AI in Personalized Medicine

Personalized medicine has become one of the most promising applications of AI in healthcare. By using patient-specific data such as genetics, lifestyle, and previous medical history, AI can help create individualized treatment plans that are more effective and have fewer side effects. This approach has been particularly beneficial in areas such as cancer treatment, where every patient's disease can behave differently.

1. **AI and Genomics in Personalized Cancer Treatment**:
   o AI plays a crucial role in **genomics**, where it analyzes genetic data to predict how cancer cells will respond to different treatments. By combining genomic data with AI, clinicians can identify mutations and tailor treatments to target specific genetic anomalies in cancer cells, improving the chances of success.
   o **Example: Foundation Medicine** offers AI-powered genomic testing to help oncologists develop personalized cancer treatments. Their AI tools analyze patients' genetic profiles to recommend therapies that are most likely to be effective, offering a more precise

169

approach than the traditional "one-size-fits-all" model.

2. **AI in Precision Medicine for Cardiovascular Diseases**:

   o AI is also helping in the development of **precision medicine** for cardiovascular diseases. By analyzing data from medical records, genetic information, and even wearable devices, AI can identify patients at risk of heart disease and suggest personalized treatment options.

   o **Example**: **HeartFlow**, an AI-driven company, uses advanced imaging and AI to analyze coronary artery disease in heart patients. The system generates a 3D model of the heart and its arteries, helping doctors determine the best course of treatment for individual patients based on their unique conditions.

3. **AI for Optimizing Drug Dosing in Personalized Medicine**:

   o AI is used to optimize **drug dosing** by analyzing patient-specific data such as age, weight, kidney function, and genetic makeup. By personalizing the dosage of medications, AI helps reduce the risk of adverse effects and improves treatment efficacy.

   o **Example**: **PHOENIX** uses AI to optimize the **dosing of cancer medications** for individual patients. The AI system calculates the optimal dose based on genetic data and the patient's response to treatment, leading to more effective therapies with fewer side effects.

4. **AI-Powered Virtual Health Assistants**:
   - Virtual health assistants powered by AI are becoming an integral part of personalized healthcare. These AI-powered systems can provide personalized health advice, track patient progress, remind patients to take medications, and even offer mental health support.
   - **Example**: **Woebot**, an AI-powered chatbot for mental health, uses natural language processing (NLP) to engage with users and offer cognitive behavioral therapy (CBT) techniques for managing anxiety and depression. Woebot personalizes its interactions based on the user's emotional state and progress, helping to provide mental health support at scale.

Summary

In this chapter, we examined the profound impact of **AI on healthcare**, highlighting how it is revolutionizing various aspects of the industry, from **diagnostics** and **treatment** to **patient care** and **drug discovery**. AI has enabled more personalized, accurate, and efficient medical practices, improving patient outcomes and reducing healthcare costs.

We explored the role of AI in **personalized medicine**, where AI tools analyze patient-specific data to recommend tailored treatments, especially in complex fields like **oncology** and **cardiology**. We also highlighted real-world examples of AI applications in healthcare, such as **Foundation Medicine's** AI-driven cancer treatments and **HeartFlow's** AI-based cardiovascular disease management.

While AI offers tremendous opportunities in healthcare, it also presents challenges, including issues related to data privacy, bias in AI models, and the need for rigorous validation of AI systems before they are widely adopted. As AI continues to advance, its role in healthcare will only grow, offering even more possibilities for improving patient care, personalizing treatments, and optimizing healthcare systems globally.

CHAPTER 18

AI in Finance: Transforming the Financial Industry

How AI is Reshaping Banking, Investment, and Insurance Sectors

Artificial Intelligence (AI) has made a profound impact on the **financial industry**, transforming the way banks, investment firms, and insurance companies operate. By automating processes, enhancing decision-making, and improving customer experiences, AI is reshaping these sectors, allowing financial institutions to offer more personalized services, streamline operations, and stay competitive in a rapidly changing environment.

1. **AI in Banking**:
    - In the banking sector, AI is being used to enhance customer service, improve fraud detection, and streamline operations. AI-powered chatbots and virtual assistants help banks provide 24/7 customer support, while machine learning algorithms detect unusual transaction patterns to identify and prevent fraud in real time.
    - **Example**: **JPMorgan Chase** uses AI in its fraud detection system to monitor credit card transactions and identify potentially fraudulent activities. AI systems analyze transaction data in real

time, flagging any unusual patterns that could indicate fraud, such as sudden large withdrawals or transactions in unexpected locations.

2. **AI in Investment**:
   o AI is revolutionizing the investment sector by improving market analysis, risk management, and portfolio optimization. By processing vast amounts of financial data, AI can identify investment opportunities, predict market trends, and suggest strategies for managing risk. These capabilities are empowering both institutional investors and individual traders to make smarter, data-driven decisions.
   o **Example**: **Goldman Sachs** uses AI and machine learning to analyze financial markets, identify trading signals, and optimize investment strategies. AI helps the firm process large volumes of data, such as economic indicators and corporate earnings reports, to identify profitable trading opportunities and minimize risks.

3. **AI in Insurance**:
   o AI is transforming the insurance industry by enabling more efficient claims processing, fraud detection, and risk assessment. Insurance companies use AI to analyze vast amounts of data—from customer profiles to weather patterns—to determine pricing, assess risk, and

personalize policies. AI also enhances customer service by automating claims processing and offering personalized recommendations.

- **Example**: **Lemonade**, an AI-driven insurance company, uses machine learning algorithms to assess insurance claims, offering rapid claims approval and personalized pricing. Lemonade's chatbot, **Maya**, guides customers through the insurance process, helping them select the best policies based on their unique needs.

The Role of AI in Financial Decision-Making

AI is playing an increasingly important role in **financial decision-making**, enabling institutions and individuals to make more informed, data-driven choices. By processing large amounts of structured and unstructured data, AI can identify patterns, predict outcomes, and optimize financial strategies.

1. **AI in Credit Scoring and Loan Approval**:
   - AI is improving the accuracy of **credit scoring** by analyzing a wider range of data points than traditional credit scoring models. By considering factors such as spending habits, social behavior, and even alternative data sources like rent payments, AI models can assess an individual's or business's creditworthiness more accurately.

- o **Example**: **Upstart**, an AI-driven lending platform, uses machine learning to assess the creditworthiness of loan applicants. By analyzing alternative data sources, such as education, work history, and financial behavior, Upstart's AI model can approve loans for individuals who might be overlooked by traditional credit scoring systems.

2. **AI in Portfolio Management and Wealth Management**:
   - o AI is enhancing **portfolio management** by providing real-time insights into market conditions, analyzing risks, and optimizing asset allocation. AI algorithms can suggest personalized investment strategies based on an individual's risk tolerance, goals, and financial situation, improving portfolio performance and diversification.
   - o **Example**: **Betterment**, a leading robo-advisor, uses AI to automatically adjust investment portfolios based on market conditions and client goals. Betterment's AI system continuously analyzes financial data and rebalances portfolios to ensure that investments align with clients' risk profiles and long-term objectives.

3. **AI in Financial Risk Management**:
   - o AI is used to identify, assess, and mitigate **financial risks**. Machine learning models can analyze large datasets to detect potential risks, such as market volatility,

interest rate fluctuations, or liquidity crises. By identifying these risks early, financial institutions can implement strategies to manage or reduce potential losses.

o **Example**: **BlackRock**, a global investment management firm, uses AI for risk management by analyzing financial data and market trends. Their AI-powered system, **Aladdin**, helps portfolio managers and risk analysts identify market shifts, assess portfolio risk, and optimize investments based on predicted financial scenarios.

4. **AI for Fraud Detection and Prevention**:

o One of the most critical applications of AI in finance is **fraud detection**. AI systems can process transaction data in real time and identify suspicious patterns that could indicate fraudulent activities, such as unusual transactions or account access. Machine learning models are continuously trained to improve their ability to detect new types of fraud and prevent financial losses.

o **Example**: **PayPal** uses AI and machine learning to detect fraudulent transactions by analyzing spending patterns and flagging suspicious activities. PayPal's system can identify potential fraud even before a transaction is completed, protecting users from unauthorized payments.

Real-World Example: AI-Powered Financial Advisors and Robo-Advisors

AI-powered **financial advisors** and **robo-advisors** are transforming wealth management by offering personalized financial advice at scale. These AI-driven platforms provide individuals with affordable, data-driven investment strategies that were once only accessible to high-net-worth individuals. Robo-advisors use algorithms to assess a client's financial situation and risk tolerance, automatically creating and managing a diversified portfolio.

1. **Betterment: AI-Powered Robo-Advisor**:
   o **Betterment** is one of the most prominent robo-advisors that uses AI to manage client portfolios. The platform offers automated investment advice, portfolio rebalancing, and tax optimization strategies based on a client's financial goals, risk tolerance, and time horizon. Betterment's AI continuously analyzes market conditions and adjusts the portfolio to ensure it aligns with the client's objectives.
   o **Example**: Betterment's AI system recommends portfolio allocations, such as stocks, bonds, and ETFs, based on an individual's preferences and financial goals. The system also automates tax-loss harvesting to optimize the client's returns by selling investments at a loss to offset gains, reducing tax liability.

2. **Wealthfront: AI-Driven Investment Management**:
    - ○ **Wealthfront** is another robo-advisor that uses AI to automate investment management. It offers services like tax-loss harvesting, portfolio rebalancing, and personalized financial planning. Wealthfront's AI algorithm ensures that clients' portfolios are diversified and optimized for long-term growth while minimizing taxes.
    - ○ **Example**: Wealthfront's **Path** feature uses AI to create a comprehensive financial plan that includes retirement savings, home purchases, and other financial goals. The system offers personalized advice based on the client's financial situation and adjusts the plan as circumstances change.
3. **Schwab Intelligent Portfolios**:
    - ○ **Schwab Intelligent Portfolios** offers a fully automated investment service, using AI to build and manage a diversified portfolio for clients. The platform offers personalized advice based on an individual's risk tolerance and investment goals. Schwab's AI model rebalances portfolios and adjusts asset allocations in response to changing market conditions.
    - ○ **Example**: Schwab's AI system uses **machine learning algorithms** to recommend an optimal mix of stocks, bonds, and other assets based on a client's

financial profile. The platform automatically rebalances the portfolio to keep it aligned with the client's goals, minimizing the need for human intervention.

4. **Robo-Advisors for Sustainable Investing**:
    o   Some robo-advisors also use AI to support **sustainable investing** by analyzing companies' environmental, social, and governance (ESG) factors. These platforms help clients invest in companies that align with their values, using AI to assess the ESG performance of potential investments.
    o   **Example**: **Ellevest**, a robo-advisor designed with women investors in mind, uses AI to create personalized portfolios that consider factors like gender, salary, and life goals. The platform also integrates **sustainable investing** strategies to help clients align their investments with their values.

Summary

In this chapter, we explored how **AI is transforming the financial industry**, particularly in the banking, investment, and insurance sectors. AI is helping financial institutions automate processes, enhance decision-making, and offer more personalized services. It is reshaping **financial decision-making**, improving

fraud detection, and making **financial planning** more accessible to a broader audience.

We also looked at **AI-powered financial advisors and robo-advisors** such as **Betterment**, **Wealthfront**, and **Schwab Intelligent Portfolios**, which use AI to automate portfolio management and offer personalized investment strategies. These platforms are democratizing access to financial advice, helping individuals make smarter investment decisions based on their unique financial goals and risk profiles.

As AI continues to evolve, its role in the financial industry will expand, enabling businesses and individuals to optimize their financial strategies, improve risk management, and achieve better outcomes. However, as with any technology, it is essential to address challenges like data privacy, security, and transparency to ensure that AI-driven financial services are reliable, secure, and fair.

CHAPTER 19

How AI is Changing Education and Learning

AI's Role in Personalized Education

Artificial Intelligence (AI) is playing an increasingly prominent role in transforming **education** by making it more personalized, accessible, and effective. AI technologies are helping educators cater to individual learning needs and offering students tailored educational experiences that were previously difficult to achieve at scale. By analyzing student data, AI can customize learning pathways, offer real-time feedback, and identify areas where students need additional support. This personalized approach to education can enhance learning outcomes, improve engagement, and help bridge gaps in knowledge.

1. **Personalized Learning Paths**:
   - AI enables **personalized learning** by creating customized learning experiences based on a student's strengths, weaknesses, preferences, and progress. Machine learning algorithms analyze a student's performance, learning style, and pace to adapt the content and pace of lessons, making it easier for students to grasp difficult concepts.
   - **Example**: Platforms like **Khan Academy** use AI to track students' progress and

recommend personalized lessons. The system adapts in real-time to student performance, offering additional practice for areas where the student is struggling and advancing them in areas where they excel.

2. **Real-Time Feedback and Assessment**:
   o One of the key advantages of AI in education is its ability to provide **real-time feedback** to students and educators. AI can assess student responses instantly, identifying mistakes and offering corrective suggestions, helping students improve their understanding as they go along. This reduces the time between learning and feedback, promoting more effective learning.
   o **Example**: AI-powered tools like **Grammarly** offer real-time grammar and writing suggestions for students, helping them refine their writing as they work. In the classroom, AI can grade assignments, quizzes, and essays more quickly and accurately than traditional methods, freeing up teachers to focus on more personalized instruction.

3. **Adaptive Learning Systems**:
   o **Adaptive learning** refers to AI systems that adjust the difficulty of tasks and content based on a student's learning progress and performance. These systems provide a tailored learning experience for each student, ensuring that content is

neither too easy nor too difficult, but just right to promote optimal learning.

- o **Example**: **DreamBox** is an AI-powered adaptive learning platform for K-8 students that customizes math lessons based on a child's learning pace. The system uses real-time data to adapt the learning experience, making sure students are always challenged but not overwhelmed.

4. **AI-Powered Tutoring**:
   - o AI-driven tutoring platforms act as **virtual tutors**, helping students understand difficult concepts and providing additional instruction outside the classroom. These systems can offer one-on-one help, answer questions, and guide students through practice problems, allowing for more individualized attention.
   - o **Example**: **Socratic by Google** is an AI-powered app that helps students solve problems and understand concepts by providing instant explanations and step-by-step solutions. It uses AI to recognize the problem and present resources or answers based on the student's question.

The Future of AI in E-Learning and Knowledge Sharing

As AI continues to evolve, its impact on **e-learning** and **knowledge sharing** will only increase, offering new ways for individuals to learn, collaborate, and share information. AI is helping create more dynamic, interactive, and engaging learning environments, while also enabling more efficient and effective knowledge management systems.

1. **AI in Virtual Classrooms and Remote Learning**:
   - AI is enhancing **virtual classrooms** by creating more engaging and interactive learning environments. Through AI-powered tools, educators can monitor student engagement, offer personalized support, and manage classroom activities more efficiently. AI also facilitates **remote learning**, making education more accessible to students anywhere in the world.
   - **Example**: **Classroom AI** tools like **Google Classroom** integrate machine learning to provide personalized feedback and recommendations to students based on their participation and performance. Additionally, AI can monitor students' engagement and attendance, ensuring that remote learning is as effective as in-person instruction.
2. **Intelligent Content Creation**:
   - AI is revolutionizing how educational content is created and distributed. With AI, educators can generate personalized learning materials based on individual student needs, offering multimedia resources such as videos, quizzes, and

interactive exercises. AI-driven systems can automatically create content based on curriculum goals and student performance, ensuring that materials are always aligned with learning objectives.

- o **Example**: **Scribe** is an AI tool that automatically generates text-based summaries, videos, and quizzes based on educational content. This tool enables educators to rapidly create learning resources tailored to the needs of their students, optimizing the learning experience and saving time.

3. **AI in Knowledge Management**:
   - o AI is transforming **knowledge sharing** by improving how information is organized, accessed, and shared within organizations or educational institutions. AI-powered knowledge management systems can automatically categorize and tag learning resources, making it easier for students and educators to find relevant materials.
   - o **Example**: **Microsoft SharePoint** and other AI-driven collaboration tools help educational institutions manage and share knowledge across departments. AI assists in content discovery, collaboration, and knowledge transfer by automatically recommending relevant articles, videos, and resources based on the user's interests and needs.

4. **Language Translation and Multilingual Learning**:

- o AI-powered language translation tools are breaking down language barriers and enabling students and educators to collaborate and access educational content in multiple languages. These tools provide real-time translations, allowing students from different linguistic backgrounds to engage in learning without limitations.
- o **Example**: **Duolingo**, an AI-powered language learning platform, uses machine learning algorithms to teach students different languages. The platform personalizes lessons based on the learner's progress and offers interactive exercises to practice speaking, writing, and listening in various languages.

Real-World Example: AI in Adaptive Learning Platforms

One of the most powerful applications of AI in education is **adaptive learning**, where AI systems adjust the content and learning pace to fit the needs of individual students. These systems provide a highly personalized learning experience, improving student outcomes and engagement by ensuring that students receive the right level of challenge and support.

1. **DreamBox**:
   - o **DreamBox** is an AI-powered platform that provides personalized math instruction to students in grades K-8. The system continuously monitors a student's

progress and adapts lessons in real time to ensure that the student is neither overwhelmed nor under-challenged. DreamBox analyzes a variety of data points, including student actions, responses, and progress, to customize learning experiences for each student.

- o **Example**: In a classroom, DreamBox adapts to the student's unique learning style, offering real-time feedback, hints, and next-step recommendations. The system adjusts difficulty levels and suggests additional lessons based on individual performance, enabling students to progress at their own pace while mastering core math concepts.

2. **Knewton**:
   - o **Knewton** is another AI-powered adaptive learning platform that tailors learning experiences based on students' strengths and weaknesses. It provides personalized learning paths and real-time feedback, helping students master concepts before moving on to more advanced material. Knewton's AI analyzes student performance and predicts the optimal learning trajectory for each student, enhancing both engagement and retention.
   - o **Example**: In **higher education**, Knewton is used by universities to deliver customized learning experiences in subjects like math, science, and

humanities. The platform offers a personalized syllabus that adapts based on how well students perform in quizzes and assignments, ensuring that they receive targeted practice where they need it most.

3. **Smart Sparrow**:
   o **Smart Sparrow** is an AI-driven platform that allows educators to design adaptive learning experiences for students. The system adjusts content based on students' real-time performance, offering personalized learning paths that address individual student needs. Smart Sparrow's AI models are used in various fields, including biology, engineering, and nursing.
   o **Example**: In **nursing education**, Smart Sparrow is used to create simulations where students can practice clinical scenarios. The AI adapts the complexity of the scenario based on the student's responses, helping students build their skills progressively in a safe and controlled environment.

4. **McGraw-Hill Education's ALEKS**:
   o **ALEKS** (Assessment and Learning in Knowledge Spaces) is an AI-powered learning platform that personalizes math and science instruction. It uses AI to assess students' knowledge and adapt the curriculum to fill any gaps in their understanding. ALEKS provides personalized practice, quizzes, and

assessments, adjusting based on each student's progress.

- o **Example**: **ALEKS** is used in middle schools, high schools, and universities to help students improve their math skills. By analyzing student performance, the platform creates a personalized learning plan and continuously adapts to ensure mastery of the material.

Summary

In this chapter, we examined the transformative role of **AI in education**, focusing on its ability to personalize learning experiences, enhance e-learning platforms, and improve knowledge sharing. AI-driven systems such as **adaptive learning platforms**, **AI-powered tutoring**, and **real-time feedback** are helping to create a more individualized, accessible, and effective education system. These systems adjust content, pace, and difficulty levels based on student performance, ensuring that each learner receives the right level of challenge and support.

We also explored **real-world examples** of AI in **adaptive learning**, including **DreamBox**, **Knewton**, and **ALEKS**, which use AI to provide personalized learning paths, real-time feedback, and dynamic content that adapts to individual student needs. These platforms have demonstrated how AI can help students achieve better outcomes by tailoring their learning experience to their unique strengths and weaknesses.

As AI continues to evolve, its applications in education will expand, offering even more opportunities for personalized learning, accessible knowledge sharing, and improved educational outcomes for students worldwide. The future of AI in education promises to make learning more effective, efficient, and engaging, helping students succeed in a rapidly changing world.

CHAPTER 20

AI in Supply Chain and Logistics

How AI Optimizes Supply Chain Management

The supply chain is a critical component of modern business operations, and AI is revolutionizing how companies manage, monitor, and optimize these complex networks. By harnessing AI, businesses can improve efficiency, reduce costs, and enhance customer satisfaction. AI technologies, such as machine learning, predictive analytics, and automation, are being applied across various stages of the supply chain to streamline operations, improve forecasting, and better allocate resources.

1. **Demand Forecasting**:
   o One of the most important functions of AI in supply chain management is **demand forecasting**. Traditional methods of forecasting rely on historical data and simple statistical models, but AI can process vast amounts of data from multiple sources, including market trends, customer preferences, and even social media sentiment, to generate more accurate demand predictions.
   o **Example**: **Walmart** uses AI to predict demand for products by analyzing customer purchase patterns, weather conditions, and social trends. This helps the company optimize inventory levels

and ensure that the right products are available in stores at the right time.

2. **Optimizing Inventory Management**:
   o AI can enhance **inventory management** by using real-time data to track stock levels, predict shortages, and optimize the ordering process. Machine learning algorithms can analyze sales data and automatically suggest inventory replenishment strategies based on current demand and supply chain dynamics.
   o **Example**: **Amazon** uses AI to manage its vast inventory of products. The company's AI system tracks inventory levels across its warehouses and adjusts stock levels based on real-time demand signals. AI-driven systems optimize the placement of products in fulfillment centers, ensuring that items are stored in the most efficient locations for faster shipping.

3. **Automation and Robotics in Warehousing**:
   o AI is also transforming warehousing through automation. **Robotic systems**, powered by AI, are being used to pick, pack, and sort items in fulfillment centers, reducing human labor and increasing efficiency. These robots are guided by AI algorithms that allow them to navigate the warehouse, identify items, and perform tasks autonomously.
   o **Example**: **Ocado**, a UK-based online grocery retailer, uses AI-powered robots

in its warehouses to optimize order picking and packing. These robots use computer vision to identify products and transport them to the appropriate packing stations, helping to increase throughput and reduce human error.

4. **Supply Chain Optimization**:
   o AI can optimize the entire supply chain by improving route planning, inventory levels, and order fulfillment. By analyzing data from suppliers, transportation systems, and warehouses, AI can recommend the most efficient ways to transport goods, balance supply and demand, and minimize delays.
   o **Example**: **UPS** uses AI to optimize its delivery routes with a system called **ORION (On-Road Integrated Optimization and Navigation)**. This AI-driven system analyzes traffic patterns, weather conditions, and delivery priorities to determine the most efficient routes for drivers, saving the company millions of dollars in fuel costs and reducing delivery times.

Predictive Analytics and AI in Logistics

Logistics is a crucial part of the supply chain that focuses on the movement of goods and services from one location to another. AI-driven **predictive analytics** is transforming logistics by helping companies anticipate future events, optimize transportation routes, and manage inventory levels. By predicting potential disruptions and demand fluctuations, businesses can proactively take action to mitigate risks and ensure smooth operations.

1. **Predicting Demand Fluctuations**:
   o Predictive analytics powered by AI enables logistics companies to anticipate changes in demand, weather conditions, or traffic patterns that may affect delivery times. By using AI to forecast demand and potential disruptions, companies can adjust their operations accordingly to avoid delays and optimize transportation costs.
   o **Example: DHL** uses AI and predictive analytics to predict fluctuations in demand, particularly during peak seasons like holidays. This allows them to adjust staffing levels, optimize warehouse space, and better plan delivery routes to handle the increased volume of shipments.
2. **Optimizing Delivery Routes**:
   o **AI in logistics** is helping companies optimize delivery routes to reduce costs, improve delivery times, and minimize environmental impact. AI-powered systems analyze real-time data, such as traffic conditions, road closures, and delivery schedules, to dynamically adjust routes and ensure timely deliveries.

- o **Example**: **FedEx** uses AI to optimize its delivery routes in real-time. The company's AI-powered system continuously analyzes traffic patterns, weather forecasts, and other data to determine the best routes for its drivers, reducing fuel consumption and delivery times while improving overall efficiency.

3. **Smart Shipment Tracking**:
   - o AI enhances **shipment tracking** by using machine learning algorithms to predict delivery times, monitor shipments, and provide real-time updates. AI-powered tracking systems can predict when goods will arrive, alerting customers and logistics teams about potential delays.
   - o **Example**: **Maersk**, a global shipping giant, uses AI-powered systems to track the movement of cargo and predict potential delays. This allows the company to proactively manage customer expectations and adjust logistics plans when needed.

4. **Supply Chain Risk Management**:
   - o AI can help logistics companies assess and manage risks by analyzing various factors such as geopolitical events, weather patterns, and supply chain disruptions. By predicting potential risks and disruptions, AI enables logistics companies to develop contingency plans and respond quickly to minimize the impact on operations.

- o **Example**: **Rolls-Royce** uses AI-powered predictive analytics to monitor its supply chain and assess risks related to the availability of parts and components. The system helps the company identify potential disruptions and take preventive measures to ensure the continuity of production.

Real-World Example: AI-Driven Inventory Management Systems

Inventory management is a critical aspect of both supply chain and logistics operations, and AI is significantly improving how businesses manage their stock levels. By analyzing historical data, market trends, and demand patterns, AI-driven inventory management systems help companies optimize stock levels, reduce waste, and improve the accuracy of demand forecasting.

1. **Amazon's AI-Powered Inventory Management**:
   - o **Amazon** is a leader in applying AI to **inventory management**. The company uses machine learning algorithms to forecast demand for millions of products across its global network of fulfillment centers. These AI systems help Amazon determine the optimal quantity of each product to keep in stock at each location, ensuring that products are readily

available to customers without overstocking.

- o **Example**: Amazon's AI-powered system predicts when and where certain products will be in demand, allowing the company to move inventory to fulfillment centers that are closest to customers. This minimizes shipping costs and delivery times, making Amazon's supply chain more efficient and responsive to customer needs.

2. **Walmart's AI-Driven Inventory Optimization**:
   - o **Walmart** uses AI to manage its inventory levels across thousands of stores and warehouses. By analyzing sales data, seasonal trends, and local preferences, Walmart's AI system helps optimize stock levels, reducing both **stockouts** and **overstocking**. This enables the company to provide better service to customers while minimizing excess inventory.
   - o **Example**: Walmart's AI-driven inventory management system ensures that popular items are always in stock by predicting demand fluctuations based on historical sales data. This system also alerts store managers to low stock levels and provides real-time data on product movement across various locations.

3. **Zara's AI-Based Inventory and Supply Chain Management**:

- o **Zara**, a leading fashion retailer, uses AI for **inventory management** and supply chain optimization. The company uses machine learning to track customer preferences, predict demand, and optimize stock levels across its global network of stores. By leveraging AI, Zara can quickly respond to fashion trends, ensuring that its inventory remains aligned with customer demand.
- o **Example**: Zara's AI system monitors sales patterns in real time, allowing the company to adjust its stock levels based on current trends. If a specific style or color is selling well, the system can automatically order more inventory, reducing the risk of stockouts and improving customer satisfaction.

4. **The Home Depot's AI-Driven Inventory System**:
   - o **The Home Depot** uses AI to optimize its **inventory management** and supply chain operations. AI algorithms analyze data on customer preferences, sales patterns, and weather forecasts to predict demand for specific products and optimize inventory levels.
   - o **Example**: During the winter season, AI-driven systems at The Home Depot forecast the demand for products like space heaters, snow shovels, and other cold-weather equipment. This allows the company to ensure that stores are

adequately stocked while avoiding overstocking, which can lead to excess inventory and waste.

Summary

In this chapter, we explored how **AI is transforming supply chain and logistics** by optimizing processes such as demand forecasting, inventory management, and route planning. AI-powered systems enable companies to automate key operations, reduce costs, improve efficiency, and provide more personalized services to customers. We discussed the role of AI in **predictive analytics**, logistics optimization, and supply chain risk management, highlighting the potential for AI to enhance decision-making and mitigate risks.

We also highlighted **real-world examples** of AI-driven inventory management systems, such as those used by **Amazon**, **Walmart**, **Zara**, and **The Home Depot**. These companies leverage AI to predict demand, optimize stock levels, and reduce waste, ultimately improving customer satisfaction and operational efficiency.

As AI continues to evolve, its potential to optimize and innovate supply chain and logistics operations will only grow, offering businesses more opportunities to improve their competitiveness and better meet the demands of customers in a dynamic global marketplace.

CHAPTER 21

AI and Creativity: The Role of AI in the Arts

AI's Role in Creative Fields such as Art, Music, and Writing

Artificial Intelligence (AI) is making waves in **creative industries**, such as **art**, **music**, and **writing**, by providing new tools that artists, musicians, and writers can use to enhance their work or even generate new creative content autonomously. AI is no longer just a tool for solving technical problems—it's now being used to push the boundaries of **creativity** itself, enabling new forms of expression and innovation in the arts.

1. **AI in Visual Arts**:
     - o AI is revolutionizing the visual arts by enabling machines to **create artwork** that mimics human creativity. Through techniques such as **deep learning** and **generative adversarial networks (GANs)**, AI can analyze vast datasets of artwork and learn how to replicate the styles of famous artists or create entirely new artistic expressions.
     - o **Example**: **AI-generated paintings** like those created by **Obvious**, a Paris-based art collective, are gaining recognition in the art world. Their AI-generated portrait,

201

Portrait of Edmond de Belamy, was sold at auction for \$432,500, highlighting how AI can be integrated into the world of art as both a tool and an artist.

2. **AI in Music Production**:
   o AI is making significant strides in the world of **music production** by assisting composers and producers in generating music, suggesting chord progressions, and even creating entire songs. AI-powered systems can analyze patterns in music, learn from a vast database of compositions, and then generate new pieces of music that mimic specific genres or styles.

   o **Example**: **OpenAI's MuseNet** and **Jukedeck** use machine learning to create original music tracks in various genres, ranging from classical to pop. MuseNet, for example, can generate compositions based on a given style, combining elements of classical music with modern pop, or even experimenting with completely new genres.

3. **AI in Writing and Storytelling**:
   o In the field of writing, AI is helping authors, journalists, and content creators by generating text, suggesting plot twists, or even producing full-length novels. AI algorithms, powered by natural language processing (NLP), can mimic writing styles and help overcome writer's block

by offering suggestions and ideas that might not have been considered.

- o **Example**: **OpenAI's GPT-3**, a state-of-the-art language model, is capable of generating human-like text. Writers use GPT-3 to generate creative writing pieces, from poetry and short stories to entire novels. The AI can even write essays or provide ideas and outlines for writers to develop further.

4. **AI in Filmmaking and Animation**:
   - o AI is also making its mark in the world of **film** and **animation** by automating tasks such as scriptwriting, animation design, and special effects creation. AI can assist filmmakers by suggesting plot structures, generating storyboards, or even creating realistic computer-generated imagery (CGI).
   - o **Example**: **Amper Music**, an AI platform, helps filmmakers and content creators produce background scores for videos and movies. The system allows creators to customize the mood, style, and tempo of the music, providing an efficient and affordable alternative to traditional music production.

How AI is Changing the Definition of Creativity

Traditionally, creativity has been viewed as a uniquely human trait, something that emerges from individual thought, inspiration, and emotional expression.

However, AI is challenging this definition by generating new content, solving creative problems, and offering suggestions that push the boundaries of what is considered creative.

1. **Collaboration Between Humans and Machines**:
   o AI is changing the concept of creativity by enabling a **collaborative** process between humans and machines. Rather than replacing human artists, musicians, and writers, AI can serve as a creative partner, providing new ideas, refining existing ones, and helping to overcome limitations. This collaboration allows creators to explore new artistic possibilities and experiment with new forms of expression.
   o **Example**: In **film production**, AI tools help filmmakers analyze scripts, suggest scene transitions, or create visual effects. Filmmakers like **Steven Spielberg** and **Ridley Scott** are using AI-driven tools in post-production to enhance storytelling, blending human creativity with AI's capacity to analyze and optimize content.

2. **AI as a Creative Tool**:
   o AI is also challenging the boundaries of what it means to create. With AI systems, the process of creation becomes more of a partnership with technology, where machines can generate ideas and assist with execution. This has sparked debates

in the art world about the **authorship** of AI-generated works and whether AI can truly be considered "creative."

- o **Example**: **The Next Rembrandt** project used AI to study the works of **Rembrandt** and create a new painting in his style. The AI analyzed data from hundreds of Rembrandt's paintings, learning his techniques, use of light, and brushstrokes. The resulting portrait, though not made by Rembrandt himself, was recognized as an artwork in his style, raising questions about the role of the artist in an age of machine-generated creativity.

3. **Expanding the Boundaries of Artistic Expression**:
   - o AI also enables the creation of entirely new art forms that were not previously possible. For example, AI can create interactive art, where the artwork changes in response to the viewer's actions, or **generative art**, where the AI creates evolving visuals that continuously change and develop over time.
   - o **Example**: **Refik Anadol**, an artist known for creating digital art with AI, uses machine learning algorithms to generate stunning visuals that blend **architecture** and **art**. His AI-powered installations, such as **Machine Hallucinations**, showcase the possibilities of using AI to create immersive art experiences that

interact with the environment and the viewer.

Real-World Example: AI-Generated Art and Music Production

AI-generated content is already making a significant impact across various creative fields. From visual art and music to writing and performance, AI is proving that it can not only complement human creativity but also open up new realms of possibility.

1. **AI-Generated Art**:
    o One of the most well-known examples of AI-generated art is **"Portrait of Edmond de Belamy"**, created by the Paris-based art collective **Obvious**. The artwork was generated using a GAN, a type of AI that learns from existing images and creates new ones. The portrait of an aristocratic figure, designed in the style of 18th-century portraits, was sold at auction for over $432,000, making it one of the most high-profile AI-generated artworks to date.
    o **Example**: **The Canvas AI** platform is another AI tool that allows users to create unique digital artwork by selecting certain parameters, such as color palettes and brushstrokes. The AI then generates original pieces of art that are personalized to the user's preferences, showcasing how

AI can democratize art creation and enable anyone to become an artist.

2. **AI in Music Production**:
   o AI has also revolutionized the music industry by helping producers create new tracks, refine compositions, and experiment with sound. AI-generated music tools, such as **Amper Music** and **AIVA (Artificial Intelligence Virtual Artist)**, are increasingly being used to compose original music for film scores, video games, and even commercial jingles.
   o **Example**: **AIVA** is an AI music composition software that has composed entire symphonies and orchestral pieces. AIVA learns from analyzing hundreds of classical music scores and uses this knowledge to create new compositions in various genres. AIVA's compositions have been performed by real orchestras, blurring the lines between human and machine-generated music.

3. **AI-Driven Music Production: OpenAI's MuseNet**:
   o **OpenAI's MuseNet** is an AI system capable of composing music in a variety of styles, from classical to contemporary genres. MuseNet can generate original compositions based on input from the user, including preferred instruments and genres. It combines machine learning with deep learning techniques to produce

music that closely mimics the styles of great composers like Mozart or contemporary artists like The Beatles.

- o **Example**: MuseNet has been used to create everything from **classical symphonies** to **pop songs**, demonstrating the flexibility of AI in the music industry. Musicians and producers use MuseNet as a tool to explore new musical ideas and enhance their creative process.

Summary

In this chapter, we explored how **AI is transforming the arts** by enabling new forms of creative expression, improving the creative process, and challenging traditional definitions of creativity. AI is playing a key role in visual arts, music production, writing, and filmmaking, offering creators new tools and possibilities to enhance their work.

AI is revolutionizing creativity by enabling collaboration between humans and machines, providing new ways for artists, musicians, and writers to generate ideas, create content, and experiment with different styles. We also examined real-world examples, such as **Obvious' AI-generated art**, **AIVA's AI-generated music**, and **MuseNet**, to demonstrate how AI is already being used in the creative industries.

As AI continues to evolve, it will increasingly become an integral part of the creative process, pushing the boundaries of what is possible in art and allowing for new, unexplored forms of creativity. Whether it's creating personalized artwork, composing music, or writing stories, AI is helping redefine what it means to be creative in the 21st century.

CHAPTER 22

AI in Legal Work: Automation in Law Firms

The Role of AI in Legal Research and Document Review

The legal profession is one of the industries where **AI** is having a profound impact, particularly in **legal research** and **document review**. Traditionally, legal research and reviewing vast amounts of legal documents were time-consuming tasks that required meticulous attention to detail and significant human effort. However, AI-powered tools are now automating these processes, allowing law firms to save time, reduce errors, and increase efficiency.

1. **AI in Legal Research**:
   - Legal research is a critical part of law practice, involving the examination of statutes, case laws, legal precedents, and other regulatory materials. AI-driven platforms have greatly simplified this process by analyzing large datasets and identifying relevant legal documents quickly. AI models can scan thousands of legal documents in seconds, providing lawyers with the information they need without having to manually sift through volumes of text.
   - **Example**: **ROSS Intelligence** is an AI-powered research tool that uses **natural**

language processing (NLP) to help lawyers find answers to legal questions quickly. ROSS reads and understands legal language, extracting the most relevant case law and statutes, allowing attorneys to spend less time on research and more on strategy.

2. **AI in Document Review**:
   - In litigation and mergers & acquisitions (M&A), document review is a time-intensive process where lawyers must analyze thousands of documents for relevant information. AI can automate this task by using machine learning algorithms to identify relevant documents based on context, keywords, and legal relevance, significantly reducing the time required for human review.
   - **Example**: **Kira Systems** is a leading AI-powered platform used by law firms to automate the review of legal documents, including contracts. By using machine learning, Kira quickly identifies critical clauses, terms, and risks in documents, helping lawyers expedite the document review process and focus on the aspects that require human expertise.

3. **Predictive Analytics for Case Outcomes**:
   - AI is increasingly being used to predict the likely outcomes of legal cases by analyzing historical data, judicial decisions, and case law. These AI tools provide lawyers with insights into how

similar cases have been decided in the past and offer predictions about the success of legal strategies.

- o **Example: Lex Machina** uses predictive analytics to give legal professionals insights into how judges and opposing counsel have ruled in past cases. This enables law firms to anticipate legal challenges and craft more effective strategies based on historical trends.

How AI is Changing the Legal Profession

AI is not only optimizing specific tasks within law firms but is also fundamentally changing the **legal profession** itself. AI technologies are enhancing law firms' ability to serve clients more efficiently, reducing operational costs, and enabling lawyers to focus on higher-value tasks like legal strategy and client relationships. As AI continues to evolve, it will continue to reshape the way legal work is performed.

1. **Automation of Routine Tasks**:
   - o One of the most significant impacts of AI is its ability to automate routine administrative tasks that have traditionally taken up a large portion of a lawyer's time. Tasks such as contract drafting, document organization, billing, and time tracking can all be streamlined through AI-powered tools, allowing lawyers to focus on more complex and value-added activities.

- o **Example**: **LegalZoom** is a platform that uses AI to help individuals and businesses automate routine legal tasks such as drafting wills, creating contracts, and registering trademarks. The service is designed to make legal processes more accessible and affordable by automating standard legal procedures.

2. **Efficiency Gains in Legal Practice**:
   - o AI can dramatically increase the **efficiency** of legal work. For instance, AI systems can quickly sort through vast amounts of legal data to identify precedents or statutes relevant to a case, freeing up lawyers to focus on interpreting and applying the law rather than spending hours on research. This leads to faster decision-making and more efficient legal processes, benefiting clients and reducing the time spent on cases.
   - o **Example**: **Ravn Systems** provides AI-based solutions for managing legal documents and contracts. Their technology helps law firms automate tasks such as document assembly, reducing the time required for these processes from hours to minutes. This allows firms to handle more cases with fewer resources.

3. **Improved Legal Services for Clients**:
   - o AI is also helping law firms deliver better services to clients by providing more

data-driven insights and offering quicker responses. With AI-powered tools, law firms can quickly analyze a client's legal needs and present them with options based on historical data, best practices, and predictive outcomes. AI is transforming the client-lawyer relationship, making legal services more accessible, transparent, and responsive.

- o **Example**: **DoNotPay**, an AI-powered chatbot, is a legal assistant that helps users with tasks such as disputing parking tickets, canceling subscriptions, and filing lawsuits. The platform uses AI to analyze legal issues and provide users with the tools and resources they need to resolve problems quickly and affordably.

4. **Access to Legal Services**:
   - o AI has the potential to democratize access to legal services by lowering the costs associated with hiring legal professionals. AI-powered platforms can offer basic legal advice, contract review, and legal document preparation at a fraction of the cost of traditional law firms, enabling individuals and small businesses to access legal assistance that they might otherwise be unable to afford.
   - o **Example**: **Rocket Lawyer** offers AI-driven legal services that allow individuals to generate documents such as leases, wills, and contracts online. The platform also provides access to legal

advice through a network of attorneys at a significantly lower cost than hiring a lawyer in person.

Real-World Example: AI-Powered Contract Analysis and Legal Assistants

One of the most impactful uses of AI in law is in **contract analysis** and the use of **AI-powered legal assistants**. AI tools are being used by law firms to help with the review, drafting, and management of contracts, improving efficiency, reducing errors, and saving significant time. Legal assistants powered by AI are also becoming more advanced, helping to answer client questions and assist lawyers in legal research, case preparation, and document management.

1. **AI-Powered Contract Analysis: Kira Systems**:
   o **Kira Systems** is an AI-powered contract analysis tool that uses machine learning to automatically identify and extract important information from legal documents, such as contracts, agreements, and financial statements. Kira can flag clauses that may require further review, such as non-compete clauses or confidentiality agreements, helping lawyers to spot potential issues faster.
   o **Example**: Law firms like **Herbert Smith Freehills** use Kira to improve the efficiency of their document review

process. The AI-powered system quickly scans contracts, extracting relevant terms and ensuring compliance with legal standards, which reduces the time spent by lawyers reviewing documents manually.

2. **AI Legal Assistants: Ross Intelligence**:
   - **ROSS Intelligence** uses **natural language processing (NLP)** and machine learning to provide AI-powered legal research and assistance. It allows legal professionals to ask questions in plain language and receive answers based on case law and legal precedents, which greatly speeds up the research process. This AI assistant can also help lawyers by suggesting relevant documents, statutes, and case law to support their arguments.
   - **Example**: Law firms like **BakerHostetler** use ROSS to assist with legal research in bankruptcy law. The AI tool helps lawyers find relevant case law and judicial opinions quickly, providing them with comprehensive insights and saving them hours of research time.

3. **AI in Contract Management: ThoughtRiver**:
   - **ThoughtRiver** is an AI tool used to review and analyze contracts, particularly for **pre-signature contract management**. It helps law firms and businesses assess the risks in contracts before they are signed by identifying

problematic clauses and potential legal risks.

- o **Example**: **Clyde & Co**, a global law firm, uses ThoughtRiver to help its clients assess and mitigate risks in contracts. The AI tool reads through contracts, provides insights into areas of concern, and helps businesses ensure that agreements align with their legal and business objectives.

Summary

In this chapter, we explored how **AI is transforming the legal profession**, particularly in **legal research**, **document review**, **contract analysis**, and the role of AI-powered **legal assistants**. AI is helping law firms automate routine tasks, improve decision-making, and streamline operations, allowing lawyers to focus on more complex and strategic aspects of legal practice.

AI-powered tools such as **Kira Systems**, **ROSS Intelligence**, and **ThoughtRiver** are already being used by law firms to enhance efficiency, reduce errors, and provide better legal services. These tools are revolutionizing how legal work is performed, enabling law firms to handle more cases, deliver faster services, and reduce costs for clients.

As AI continues to evolve, its role in law will continue to expand, potentially reshaping the profession entirely. With further advancements in AI, the future of legal work will likely involve greater collaboration between lawyers and AI tools, ensuring that legal services are more efficient, accessible, and affordable than ever before.

CHAPTER 23

The Impact of AI on Labor Markets and Employment

How AI is Reshaping Labor Markets Globally

The rise of Artificial Intelligence (AI) is dramatically reshaping labor markets around the world. AI technologies, ranging from machine learning algorithms to robotic process automation, are transforming industries and creating new ways of working. While AI has the potential to drive economic growth and increase productivity, it is also introducing profound changes to the structure of the workforce, affecting employment patterns, job types, and required skill sets.

1. **AI-Driven Transformation Across Sectors**:
   o AI is influencing various sectors, including **manufacturing**, **healthcare**, **finance**, and **retail**, by automating tasks, streamlining operations, and improving decision-making. In sectors like finance and healthcare, AI can process vast amounts of data and generate insights that humans might overlook, leading to more informed decisions and better outcomes. However, in more manual sectors like manufacturing and logistics, AI and automation are rapidly replacing routine and repetitive jobs.

- Example: In **banking**, AI is revolutionizing customer service with chatbots and virtual assistants, reducing the need for call center workers but creating opportunities for those skilled in developing and managing AI systems. Similarly, **healthcare** is seeing AI-driven tools like diagnostic algorithms and robotic surgery assistants, which are changing the roles of doctors, nurses, and medical technicians.

2. **Global Disparities and Regional Impacts**:
   - The impact of AI on labor markets is not uniform globally. Developed economies, such as those in the **United States**, **Germany**, and **Japan**, are seeing rapid AI adoption in industries that require high technical skills, leading to the creation of new high-skill job opportunities. However, developing countries and those with large populations engaged in low-skill, manual labor jobs may experience higher risks of job displacement, particularly in industries like agriculture and textiles.
   - Example: In countries like **India** and **China**, manufacturing industries are being significantly impacted by AI-driven automation in factories, resulting in job losses for low-skilled workers. At the same time, demand for **AI specialists**, **data scientists**, and **engineers** is increasing, creating a **digital divide** that

benefits those with access to education and technology.

3. **Changing Workforce Demands**:
   o As AI continues to evolve, labor markets are experiencing a **shift in the types of skills** that are in demand. High-tech roles in fields like **data science, robotics**, and **software engineering** are seeing exponential growth. Conversely, there is a decline in demand for low-skilled, repetitive jobs, which AI and automation can perform more efficiently.
   o **Example**: The **World Economic Forum** predicts that by 2025, **automation** could replace 85 million jobs globally, while creating 97 million new roles—particularly in fields related to **data analysis, AI management**, and **cybersecurity**. This shift emphasizes the importance of **re-skilling** and **upskilling** workers to meet new job requirements.

The Challenges of Job Displacement and Upskilling

AI's ability to automate a wide range of tasks, from customer service to warehouse management, has led to concerns about **job displacement** and the need for workers to acquire new skills. While AI can create new job opportunities, the transition for workers who lose their jobs to automation can be challenging.

1. **Job Displacement**:

○ As AI systems become capable of performing tasks that were once done by humans—such as data entry, driving, and even complex problem-solving—many workers find their roles becoming redundant. This leads to **job displacement**, particularly for those in industries where routine tasks can be automated. Manufacturing, retail, and logistics are among the hardest-hit sectors, where workers may face unemployment if they are unable to transition to new roles.

○ **Example**: The rise of **self-checkout systems** in supermarkets and retail stores has led to the displacement of cashiers. While automation increases efficiency, it also leads to job losses for individuals in low-skill positions, contributing to growing income inequality.

2. **The Upskilling and Reskilling Challenge**:

○ **Upskilling** and **reskilling** are essential strategies for addressing job displacement caused by AI. Workers in industries at risk of automation need opportunities to acquire new skills in fields that are less likely to be automated, such as **AI development**, **healthcare**, and **creative industries**. Governments, businesses, and educational institutions must collaborate to provide accessible training programs that equip workers with the skills needed for the jobs of the future.

- o **Example**: Companies like **Amazon** are investing heavily in reskilling initiatives to help employees transition into new roles. Amazon's **Upskilling 2025** program aims to provide training for 100,000 workers, helping them gain skills in areas like cloud computing and AI, which are expected to remain in demand as automation increases.

3. **Worker Displacement in Low-Skill Jobs**:
   - o Workers in low-skill jobs, particularly those in manufacturing, warehousing, and customer service, are often the most vulnerable to displacement. The rapid adoption of AI technologies in these sectors has resulted in **job loss** without clear pathways for these workers to transition into new roles.
   - o **Example**: **Foxconn**, a major supplier to companies like **Apple**, has invested heavily in automation to replace workers in its Chinese factories. The company has implemented AI-driven robots for tasks like assembly, reducing its workforce by hundreds of thousands of employees. While this increases productivity, it has also left many workers without a clear alternative.

4. **AI and Job Creation**:
   - o On the other hand, AI is also creating **new job opportunities** in fields such as **data science**, **AI engineering**, and **robotics**. As AI and automation become more

integrated into business operations, the demand for workers with specialized skills in these areas will continue to grow. These new roles often require **advanced education** and **technical expertise**, which presents both a challenge and an opportunity for the workforce.

- o **Example**: **AI research and development** are creating job opportunities for **AI engineers**, **data scientists**, and **machine learning specialists**. In countries like the **United States** and **Germany**, demand for AI-related positions is growing, creating a **talent gap** that companies are working to fill.

Real-World Example: The Rise of Automation and Its Effects on Manufacturing Jobs

One of the industries most affected by AI and automation is **manufacturing**. Over the past few decades, industrial automation has already replaced many manual labor jobs. With the introduction of **AI-driven robotics** and **machine learning** in manufacturing processes, the pace of automation has only increased, creating significant disruptions in labor markets.

1. **The Automotive Industry**:
   - o The **automotive industry** is a prime example of how automation, driven by AI, has transformed manufacturing. AI

and robotics have replaced many of the manual labor tasks traditionally performed by human workers, from assembly lines to quality control. While automation has increased efficiency and reduced costs, it has also resulted in a decrease in the number of workers needed on the factory floor.

o **Example**: **Tesla**, a leader in electric vehicle production, has heavily invested in automation. The company uses AI-powered robots to perform tasks like assembling car parts, welding, and painting. While automation has enabled Tesla to produce cars more quickly and with fewer defects, it has also led to job losses in traditional manufacturing roles.

2. **Job Losses in Low-Skill Roles**:

o In industries like **textiles, food processing,** and **electronics manufacturing**, AI-driven automation has replaced many **low-skill jobs**. Workers who once performed repetitive tasks like sewing, packaging, or sorting are now being replaced by AI-powered robots that can perform these tasks more efficiently.

o **Example**: **Foxconn,** a major manufacturer of electronic devices, has implemented AI-powered robots in its factories. The company's decision to replace thousands of workers with robots has raised concerns about **job**

displacement in countries where manufacturing jobs were a significant source of employment.

3. **Reskilling Programs in Manufacturing**:
    o As automation continues to displace jobs in manufacturing, companies and governments are focusing on **reskilling programs** to help workers transition to new roles. For example, in the **UK**, there are initiatives to provide retraining for workers in sectors at risk of automation, helping them gain skills in fields like **AI programming**, **robotics maintenance**, and **data analysis**.
    o **Example**: **BMW** has implemented a reskilling program for its factory workers to help them transition into roles that involve working alongside AI-powered systems. These workers are trained in areas such as **robotic programming** and **machine learning** to ensure that they remain valuable assets in the AI-driven manufacturing environment.

Summary

In this chapter, we explored how **AI is reshaping global labor markets**, particularly in sectors like **manufacturing**, **customer service**, and **logistics**. While AI is driving **economic growth** and creating new job opportunities, it is also leading to **job**

displacement—especially for workers in low-skill, repetitive roles. The rise of **automation** is causing significant disruptions in industries like **automotive manufacturing** and **electronics**, where AI-powered robots are replacing human labor.

We also discussed the importance of **upskilling** and **reskilling** workers to help them transition into new roles in AI-related fields such as **data science**, **robotics**, and **AI engineering**. Programs like **Amazon's Upskilling 2025** initiative and reskilling efforts in the **automotive industry** are examples of how companies are preparing workers for the AI-driven workforce of the future.

As AI continues to evolve, its impact on labor markets will only deepen. To ensure that the benefits of AI are widely shared, it is essential to address the challenges of **job displacement**, **income inequality**, and **access to education** through thoughtful policy and investment in workforce development.

CHAPTER 24

Addressing the Ethical Challenges of AI in the Workplace

Tackling AI-Driven Job Displacement, Bias, and Fairness

As **Artificial Intelligence (AI)** continues to make significant inroads into the workplace, it brings both transformative benefits and ethical challenges. While AI can enhance productivity and efficiency, its rapid adoption also raises concerns regarding **job displacement**, **bias**, and **fairness**. These issues are particularly critical as organizations adopt AI tools for hiring, performance evaluation, and workplace management.

1. **AI-Driven Job Displacement**:
    o AI has the potential to automate many tasks traditionally performed by humans, leading to significant changes in the labor market. **Job displacement** occurs when tasks that were once carried out by workers are automated through AI systems, which could lead to job losses, especially in low-skill and repetitive roles.
    o **Example**: In **manufacturing** and **customer service**, AI-driven automation is replacing workers. For example, **Amazon's** use of robots in warehouses to perform sorting and packing tasks has led

to the reduction of low-skill jobs in these areas, raising concerns about the future of employment for these workers. To address this, companies must implement strategies to reskill and upskill workers for the AI-driven workforce.

2. **Bias in AI Systems**:
   o AI systems are only as unbiased as the data they are trained on. If AI systems are trained on biased data—whether it be historical hiring data or biased customer feedback—there is a risk that the systems may perpetuate existing biases, leading to unfair decision-making. **Bias in AI** can affect hiring, promotions, and workplace evaluations, reinforcing inequality and discrimination.
   o **Example**: In recruitment, AI-powered tools that assess resumes and conduct initial job screenings have been found to exhibit bias based on gender, race, or age. In 2018, **Amazon** scrapped its AI-powered hiring tool because it was found to be biased against women, as it was trained on data that favored resumes submitted by male candidates. This example underscores the need for rigorous testing and continuous monitoring of AI systems to ensure fairness and equity in decision-making.

3. **Ensuring Fairness in AI**:
   o To tackle issues of **fairness**, companies need to ensure that AI systems are

designed, tested, and implemented in ways that promote equal treatment and opportunities for all employees. This includes actively addressing biases in data, ensuring transparency in AI algorithms, and embedding fairness into the design and deployment process.

- o **Example**: **Fairness constraints** can be incorporated into AI models to ensure that they do not disadvantage any particular group. For instance, AI-driven recruitment platforms can be designed to screen for gender-neutral language and ensure that hiring decisions are based on skills and qualifications rather than biased data patterns.

Legal, Ethical, and Social Challenges in AI Adoption

The integration of AI into the workplace presents **legal**, **ethical**, and **social challenges** that companies must address to ensure responsible use of AI. These challenges encompass issues of **data privacy**, **transparency**, **accountability**, and **employee rights**.

1. **Data Privacy and Protection**:
   - o One of the primary ethical challenges in AI adoption is ensuring that employee data is handled with care and in compliance with data protection regulations. AI systems often rely on large amounts of personal data, which can raise concerns about privacy violations if

the data is mishandled or used without consent.

- o **Example**: In the European Union, the **General Data Protection Regulation (GDPR)** imposes strict rules on how companies can collect, store, and use employee data, including data used in AI systems. Companies must obtain explicit consent from employees to use their data in AI-driven processes and provide transparency regarding how their data is being used, ensuring that it is not exploited or misused.

2. **Accountability and Transparency**:
   - o As AI systems make increasingly important decisions regarding hiring, promotions, and performance evaluations, companies must ensure that there is accountability and **transparency** in how these decisions are made. Employees and candidates should have a clear understanding of how AI systems work and how decisions are being derived.
   - o **Example**: A **facial recognition AI system** used for employee monitoring could raise concerns about accountability, especially if the system makes decisions about access to certain areas or privileges based on the recognition of facial features. In such cases, transparency regarding how these decisions are made, and who is responsible for the system's

actions, is crucial to prevent misuse and ensure fairness.

3. **Employee Rights and Job Security**:
   - The rise of AI also brings concerns about **employee rights**, particularly as automation leads to job displacement or changes in the nature of work. Employees may feel insecure about their jobs and roles in an increasingly AI-driven workplace, and this can lead to issues around job security, job satisfaction, and the future of work.
   - **Example**: Employees working in roles that are highly susceptible to automation may feel threatened by AI and uncertain about their job prospects. Employers should take proactive steps to communicate their AI adoption strategies transparently and ensure that employees are not left behind through initiatives like **job transition programs**, **re-skilling**, and **career development opportunities**.

4. **The Social Impact of AI on Employment**:
   - The **social impact** of AI on employment is another important consideration. The widespread implementation of AI and automation may lead to societal shifts, including economic inequality, unemployment, and the need for broader societal interventions to mitigate these effects. Governments, businesses, and educators must work together to ensure

that AI-driven changes do not exacerbate existing social inequalities.

- **Example**: In countries with high levels of low-skill, manual labor, AI adoption can have disproportionate social consequences. In **India**, for instance, a large portion of the population works in the manufacturing and service industries, where automation is increasingly replacing human workers. The social implications of AI adoption in these regions include the risk of **economic displacement** and the widening gap between those who have access to AI-driven job opportunities and those who do not.

Real-World Example: AI in Workplace Surveillance and Privacy Concerns

AI is increasingly being used for **workplace surveillance**, where employers monitor employee behavior and performance using AI-driven systems. While these tools can improve productivity and ensure workplace safety, they also raise significant privacy and ethical concerns, particularly regarding the extent to which employee actions are tracked and analyzed.

1. **AI in Employee Monitoring**:
   - AI-powered systems are being used to monitor employees in a variety of ways, such as tracking their work hours, performance, email usage, and even

physical movements within office spaces. This level of surveillance raises questions about employee privacy and the potential for misuse.

- o **Example**: **Amazon** has been criticized for using AI-powered cameras in delivery vans to monitor drivers' speeds, driving habits, and even facial expressions to assess their mood. While this helps Amazon ensure that drivers are performing their jobs efficiently, it also raises concerns about the **intrusiveness** of such surveillance and the impact it may have on workers' autonomy and well-being.

2. **Privacy Concerns in AI Surveillance**:
   - o AI-driven surveillance tools can also track sensitive personal data, such as employees' locations, behavior patterns, and even their emotional states. Without proper oversight, this can lead to privacy violations and abuse of personal information.
   - o **Example**: **Clearview AI** has faced significant backlash for using facial recognition technology to gather public images of people without their consent, which is then used to track individuals' activities in the workplace or public spaces. The lack of transparency in how data is collected and used, and the absence of clear employee consent, has raised

concerns about the ethical implications of such AI surveillance technologies.

3. **Balancing Efficiency with Employee Privacy**:
   o Employers must strike a delicate balance between using AI for **increased productivity** and **efficiency** while respecting employee privacy and ensuring that surveillance does not overreach. Transparency about the use of AI in monitoring employees, clear consent protocols, and safeguards to prevent misuse are crucial to maintaining ethical standards in AI adoption.
   o **Example**: **Microsoft** uses AI-powered tools in its office environments to monitor employee well-being and productivity but emphasizes that its systems are designed with privacy and transparency in mind. The company has put in place clear guidelines for data usage and ensures that employees are aware of how their data is being collected and monitored.

Summary

In this chapter, we discussed the **ethical challenges** of AI in the workplace, particularly focusing on **job displacement**, **bias**, **fairness**, **data privacy**, and **employee rights**. As AI continues to automate tasks and processes, it raises important questions about how businesses can ensure fairness, transparency, and accountability. We also explored **real-world examples** of AI-powered tools in **workplace surveillance** and the privacy concerns associated with these systems, highlighting the ethical considerations that need to be addressed when deploying AI in the workplace.

To mitigate the challenges of job displacement, organizations must focus on **upskilling and reskilling** their workforce, offering support for workers whose roles are at risk of automation. Moreover, addressing **bias** in AI systems and ensuring that AI-powered decisions are made fairly and transparently is crucial to preventing discrimination and promoting equality.

As AI continues to shape the workplace, it is essential that organizations adopt responsible and ethical practices in the development and implementation of AI systems, ensuring that the benefits of AI are realized without compromising employee rights, privacy, or fairness.

CHAPTER 25

Regulation and Policy: Governing AI in the Workforce

The Need for Regulation in AI-Driven Work Environments

As AI technologies become more pervasive in the workplace, there is an increasing need for **regulation** to ensure that AI is deployed in a way that is ethical, fair, and beneficial for both workers and employers. The rapid adoption of AI tools in work environments—ranging from automated decision-making in hiring and promotion to AI-powered monitoring of employees—raises significant questions about workers' rights, privacy, job security, and the fairness of AI systems.

1. **Protecting Workers' Rights**:
    - As AI tools become integral to the workplace, they can sometimes infringe upon workers' rights, particularly in areas like **privacy**, **discrimination**, and **surveillance**. Without clear regulations in place, AI systems might be used in ways that violate employee rights or contribute to unjust outcomes.
    - **Example**: AI-powered systems for monitoring employee productivity—such as the ones used by **Amazon** to track delivery drivers—have raised concerns about surveillance, transparency, and the

237

potential for **invasions of privacy**. Workers may feel uncomfortable or pressured by these systems if they are not regulated properly, leading to a toxic work environment.

2. **Ensuring Fairness in AI Decision-Making**:
   o Another key challenge of AI in the workplace is **bias**. AI systems can perpetuate and even exacerbate biases in decision-making, especially if they are trained on biased historical data. Without regulation to address fairness and prevent discrimination, AI-driven systems could unfairly disadvantage certain demographic groups.
   o **Example**: In recruitment, AI algorithms that assess resumes and job applications may inherit biases present in the historical hiring data, leading to discrimination against women, minorities, or other underrepresented groups. Regulating how AI systems are trained and tested for fairness can help mitigate these risks and ensure that AI tools are used to promote equality in hiring and promotion.

3. **Promoting Transparency and Accountability**:
   o **Transparency** in AI processes and decisions is critical to ensuring that workers and employers understand how AI systems are making decisions that impact employment. Without clear rules around transparency, workers may have little understanding of why certain

decisions—such as hiring rejections, promotions, or performance evaluations—are being made by AI systems.

- o **Example**: AI systems used in performance evaluations might make decisions based on factors that employees don't understand or agree with, such as algorithmic judgments of work patterns or behavior. **Accountability** measures need to be in place to ensure that AI systems are functioning as intended and that companies are held responsible for the consequences of AI-driven decisions.

4. **Addressing Job Displacement**:
   - o **AI-driven automation** is expected to displace many jobs, especially those involving routine, repetitive tasks. Regulation must address the **social and economic** impact of job losses caused by AI, providing safety nets for displaced workers and facilitating **job transition programs**.
   - o **Example**: As automation systems replace manual labor in manufacturing, retail, and logistics, there needs to be legislation to ensure that displaced workers have access to retraining programs and job placement assistance, as well as financial support during the transition.

How Governments Are Addressing AI in the Workforce

Governments around the world are beginning to recognize the need for **AI regulation** and are starting to introduce laws and policies aimed at managing the integration of AI technologies into the workforce. These regulations aim to balance the benefits of AI innovation with the protection of workers' rights, ensuring that AI adoption does not disproportionately harm certain groups or undermine social stability.

1. **AI Regulation Frameworks**:
   - Many countries are developing **AI regulation frameworks** to address the ethical and legal issues posed by AI. These frameworks focus on ensuring that AI systems are safe, fair, and transparent, and that workers are protected from potential harm. Countries like the **European Union**, **China**, and the **United States** are working to create comprehensive regulations that balance the development of AI technologies with the protection of individual rights and labor markets.
   - **Example**: In the **United States**, the **National Artificial Intelligence Initiative Act** was signed into law in 2020 to guide AI research and development across federal agencies. While the initiative emphasizes innovation and leadership in AI, it also promotes **ethical AI** practices, including

fairness and transparency in AI decision-making.

2. **AI in the Workforce Policies**:
   o Governments are also creating policies specifically aimed at managing AI's impact on the workforce. These policies focus on addressing issues like **job displacement, reskilling**, and the **future of work**. By facilitating job transition programs, providing training for future skills, and addressing income inequality, governments aim to ensure that AI adoption is beneficial for all sectors of society.
   o **Example**: **South Korea** has implemented initiatives to help workers who are affected by automation in the manufacturing industry. The government's **AI-based reskilling programs** focus on helping workers acquire new skills in emerging sectors such as **AI programming, robotics**, and **big data analytics**.

3. **International Cooperation on AI Ethics**:
   o AI adoption and its impact on labor markets are global issues that require international collaboration. Governments and international bodies are working together to establish **global AI standards** and ethical guidelines that ensure AI is used responsibly and equitably across borders. This is particularly important given the cross-border nature of AI

technologies and their potential to impact workers worldwide.

- **Example**: The **OECD (Organisation for Economic Co-operation and Development)** has created the **OECD Principles on AI**, which emphasize responsible AI development, transparency, accountability, and the protection of workers. These principles provide guidance for governments to create AI policies that promote innovation while safeguarding workers' rights.

Real-World Example: The European Union's AI Regulations and Workforce Impact

The **European Union (EU)** has been at the forefront of regulating AI, with the aim of ensuring that AI technologies are developed and deployed in a way that benefits both innovation and society. The EU's regulatory framework seeks to address the challenges posed by AI in the workforce, particularly the ethical implications of AI in decision-making, surveillance, and employment.

1. **EU's Artificial Intelligence Act**:
   - The **European Commission** proposed the **Artificial Intelligence Act** in 2021, aiming to regulate AI technologies within the EU. The Act sets out requirements for AI systems based on the level of risk they pose, with stricter regulations for high-risk AI applications, including those used

in hiring, surveillance, and law enforcement.

- o **Example**: AI systems used in hiring or job performance evaluations would fall under high-risk categories, requiring companies to ensure that their AI systems are fair, transparent, and explainable. This means that companies must ensure that AI-driven decisions in recruitment are non-discriminatory and that employees can appeal AI-based decisions.

2. **AI and Worker Rights in the EU**:
   - o The EU's regulatory approach also addresses **workers' rights** by ensuring that AI systems used in the workplace comply with **labor laws** and respect **privacy**. For example, AI-driven workplace surveillance and monitoring systems must be implemented with clear guidelines and transparency to prevent violations of employees' rights.
   - o **Example**: The **GDPR (General Data Protection Regulation)** plays a critical role in ensuring that AI systems that process employee data comply with strict data protection standards. This includes ensuring that employees' data is only used for legitimate purposes, that it is processed transparently, and that employees have the right to access and control their personal data.

3. **Impact on Job Displacement and Reskilling**:

- The EU is also focused on mitigating the impact of AI-driven job displacement through **reskilling initiatives** and policies that promote job transition. The EU has allocated funds to support worker training programs in AI, digital skills, and future-proof jobs, ensuring that employees whose jobs are at risk of automation have access to the skills and resources they need to transition into new roles.
- **Example**: The EU's **Digital Education Action Plan** aims to equip workers with the skills necessary for the AI-powered workforce of the future. This includes initiatives for **upskilling** in areas such as data analysis, AI programming, and cybersecurity.

Summary

In this chapter, we examined the importance of **regulation** in managing the integration of **AI** into the workforce. As AI technologies continue to shape work environments, there is a growing need for **legal, ethical, and social frameworks** that address challenges such as **job displacement**, **bias**, **fairness**, **privacy**, and **workers' rights**. Governments worldwide are recognizing the need for regulation and are introducing policies to guide AI development while protecting workers and promoting fairness.

The **European Union's AI regulations** provide a real-world example of how governments are addressing these challenges, with comprehensive laws aimed at ensuring **AI fairness**, **data privacy**, and **worker protection**. The **EU Artificial Intelligence Act** and **GDPR** are shaping the future of AI deployment in the workplace, helping organizations adopt AI responsibly and ensuring that workers are not left behind as automation and AI transform industries.

As AI continues to evolve, it is crucial for governments, businesses, and international bodies to collaborate on creating effective regulations that foster innovation while protecting the rights and well-being of the workforce.

CHAPTER 26

AI for Social Good: Leveraging Technology for Positive Impact

Using AI to Tackle Social Issues Like Poverty, Inequality, and Climate Change

Artificial Intelligence (AI) is often associated with enhancing business efficiency and driving innovation in tech industries. However, AI's potential goes far beyond these areas. In recent years, **AI for social good** has emerged as a powerful tool to tackle some of the world's most pressing challenges, such as **poverty**, **inequality**, and **climate change**. By harnessing the power of data and machine learning, AI can help create solutions that improve living conditions, promote social equity, and address environmental issues.

1. **AI in Poverty Alleviation**:
    o   AI has the potential to significantly contribute to efforts to alleviate **poverty** by improving access to resources, increasing economic opportunities, and enhancing the effectiveness of poverty-targeted programs. For instance, AI can be used to **analyze economic data** to identify regions or populations at risk of poverty, and predictive analytics can help governments and organizations deliver aid to those who need it most.

o **Example**: **The World Bank** has leveraged AI and big data analytics to **identify vulnerable populations** in developing countries. By analyzing factors such as income levels, access to healthcare, and education, AI models can predict areas most at risk for poverty and direct resources and aid accordingly. This targeted approach ensures that help reaches those who need it the most.

2. **AI in Addressing Inequality**:

   o **Inequality**—whether economic, racial, or gender-based—remains one of the world's most significant challenges. AI can play a crucial role in addressing these disparities by providing tools for more equitable decision-making and resource distribution. AI systems can help identify **biases** in hiring practices, access to services, and education, allowing for more inclusive and fair policies.

   o **Example**: **AI-powered recruitment platforms** are increasingly being used to reduce gender and racial bias in hiring. Companies like **HireVue** and **Pymetrics** use AI to analyze job applicants based on their skills, competencies, and experiences rather than unconscious biases or personal characteristics like gender or race. These tools are helping promote more diverse and inclusive hiring practices.

3. **AI in Tackling Climate Change**:

- AI is being leveraged in the fight against **climate change** to improve environmental monitoring, optimize energy use, and reduce carbon footprints. AI can analyze large datasets related to energy consumption, weather patterns, and carbon emissions to develop strategies for reducing environmental impact and mitigating climate change.
- **Example**: **Google's DeepMind** has partnered with energy companies to use AI for optimizing energy use in data centers. By using AI to predict and manage energy consumption, Google has significantly reduced its carbon footprint, helping the company achieve its goal of **running data centers on renewable energy**. Similarly, AI is used to model climate change and predict the impact of environmental policies, aiding governments and organizations in making more informed decisions to protect the planet.

AI's Potential to Address Global Challenges

AI's ability to process and analyze large amounts of data allows it to address **global challenges** in ways that were previously unimaginable. By leveraging AI, organizations and governments can create data-driven solutions that are scalable, sustainable, and effective in solving complex problems across the globe.

1. **AI in Healthcare**:
   o AI has the potential to transform **healthcare** by making diagnoses faster, more accurate, and more accessible to underserved populations. AI-powered tools can assist doctors in diagnosing diseases, predicting patient outcomes, and personalizing treatments. Additionally, AI can help address **healthcare disparities** by improving access to quality care in remote or impoverished areas.
   o **Example**: **IBM Watson Health** uses AI to assist healthcare providers with decision-making by analyzing medical data and providing personalized treatment recommendations. AI is also being used in **global health initiatives** to track the spread of diseases like **Ebola** and **COVID-19**, predict outbreaks, and allocate resources more effectively.

2. **AI in Education**:
   o AI can make **education** more accessible and equitable by providing personalized learning experiences and supporting educators in identifying the specific needs of their students. AI-powered tools can help overcome barriers such as language, geography, and income, ensuring that quality education is available to all, regardless of background.
   o **Example**: **Khan Academy's AI-driven platform** offers personalized learning

experiences for students worldwide, adapting content to the learner's pace and level. AI tools in education can also help **bridge the digital divide**, ensuring that students in remote or underserved areas have access to the same high-quality education as their peers in urban centers.

3. **AI in Sustainable Development**:
   o AI can support efforts to achieve the **United Nations Sustainable Development Goals (SDGs)**, which aim to address poverty, inequality, climate change, and other critical global challenges. AI applications in sectors such as **agriculture**, **water management**, and **urban planning** can optimize resources and contribute to more sustainable and equitable development.
   o **Example**: **Agri-Tech** companies are using AI to **optimize crop yields**, reduce water usage, and ensure sustainable agricultural practices. AI tools help farmers make data-driven decisions about planting, irrigation, and harvesting, which leads to higher productivity and more sustainable farming practices.

Real-World Example: AI in Disaster Relief and Humanitarian Aid

One of the most impactful ways AI is being used for social good is in **disaster relief** and **humanitarian aid**. AI technologies can help **predict natural disasters**,

analyze damage, and **optimize resource distribution**, ensuring that aid reaches those in need as quickly as possible. In the aftermath of disasters, AI can provide real-time insights into affected areas, helping rescue teams prioritize their efforts and direct resources efficiently.

1. **AI in Disaster Prediction and Response**:
   o AI can help predict and mitigate the effects of natural disasters by analyzing historical data, weather patterns, and real-time satellite images. Machine learning models can identify potential threats such as hurricanes, earthquakes, and floods, providing early warnings to those in danger and helping governments and humanitarian organizations prepare accordingly.
   o **Example**: The **Red Cross** uses AI-powered systems to **predict and manage disaster response**. For instance, AI systems analyze satellite imagery and weather data to predict areas most likely to be affected by floods, helping aid organizations plan their response and allocate resources to the most vulnerable areas. AI tools also help assess damage in the aftermath of a disaster by analyzing aerial images and social media posts, allowing rescue teams to identify areas that need immediate attention.
2. **AI in Refugee and Migrant Assistance**:

- o AI is also being used to support refugees and displaced persons, helping them find **safe routes**, access healthcare, and secure essential services. By analyzing data from various sources, AI can help humanitarian organizations provide targeted support to those who need it most, ensuring that resources are distributed effectively.
- o **Example**: **UNHCR (United Nations High Commissioner for Refugees)** uses AI to track the movements of refugees and identify potential risks they face along their journey. AI tools help provide critical information about border crossings, access to shelters, and availability of food and medical assistance.

3. **AI in Humanitarian Aid Logistics**:
- o AI is improving the **logistics of humanitarian aid**, ensuring that food, medicine, and supplies are distributed to the right locations at the right time. AI-powered tools can predict where resources will be needed most, manage supply chains, and optimize the distribution of aid to avoid shortages or waste.
- o **Example: The World Food Programme (WFP)** uses AI to manage its supply chains and predict food shortages in areas affected by conflict or disaster. By analyzing satellite imagery, weather patterns, and socio-economic data, AI

helps the WFP ensure that food aid is delivered efficiently and effectively, reducing delays and preventing hunger.

Summary

In this chapter, we explored how **AI for social good** is being used to tackle some of the world's most pressing challenges, such as **poverty, inequality**, and **climate change**. From addressing global healthcare disparities to creating more sustainable agricultural practices, AI is transforming how we approach social issues and making a positive impact on communities worldwide. AI has the potential to improve **education, healthcare**, and **sustainable development**, providing opportunities for marginalized populations and ensuring a more equitable future.

We also examined **real-world examples**, such as the **use of AI in disaster relief and humanitarian aid**. AI is being leveraged to predict natural disasters, assess damage, and optimize the distribution of resources, helping organizations like the **Red Cross** and **UNHCR** provide timely support to those in need.

As AI continues to evolve, its ability to drive social change will only grow. However, for AI to truly be used for social good, it is essential that it is deployed responsibly, with consideration for ethical implications and a focus on **equity** and **fairness**. By harnessing the power of AI, we can create solutions that not only improve individual lives but also address global challenges and promote a better future for all.

CHAPTER 27

Preparing for the Future: How to Adapt to AI in the Workplace

Practical Strategies for Professionals to Thrive in an AI-Driven Workforce

As **Artificial Intelligence (AI)** continues to shape the modern workforce, professionals across industries must be prepared to adapt to the changes AI brings. While AI is transforming many aspects of work, it also presents opportunities for those willing to embrace new tools, learn new skills, and stay ahead of technological advancements. For professionals, the key to thriving in an AI-driven workforce lies in understanding how AI will impact their roles, and developing the skills and mindset necessary to work effectively alongside AI systems.

1. **Embrace AI as a Tool for Augmentation, Not Replacement**:
   - The most successful professionals in the AI-driven future will see AI not as a threat but as a tool to augment their skills and enhance their productivity. Instead of competing with AI, professionals should leverage AI systems to handle routine tasks, automate workflows, and provide insights, allowing them to focus on more creative, strategic, or interpersonal aspects of their jobs.

255

- o **Example**: In fields like **marketing**, AI tools can be used for data analysis and content personalization, enabling marketers to focus on creative campaigns and client engagement. Similarly, in **law**, AI can assist with legal research and document review, freeing up lawyers to focus on more complex legal strategies and client consultations.

2. **Develop Interdisciplinary Skills**:
   - o While technical skills in **AI development**, **data analysis**, and **machine learning** will be essential for many roles, the ability to **collaborate** and work alongside AI is just as important. Professionals should develop **interdisciplinary skills** that combine **domain expertise** with an understanding of how AI can be used to improve workflows in their field.
   - o **Example**: A **healthcare professional** may need to understand AI-driven diagnostic tools, but they also need strong **communication skills** to explain complex AI-generated insights to patients. Similarly, a **project manager** may not need to be an expert in AI, but they should be able to oversee AI-driven projects and work with AI specialists to integrate the technology into their workflows.

3. **Focus on Creativity, Critical Thinking, and Emotional Intelligence**:

- ○ AI excels at tasks that involve repetitive work, pattern recognition, and data analysis, but it cannot replicate **human creativity**, **critical thinking**, and **emotional intelligence**. Professionals who focus on developing these uniquely human skills will continue to add value in an AI-driven workplace. Emphasizing **problem-solving**, **decision-making**, and **collaboration** will help individuals thrive in roles that require complex, judgment-based decisions and interpersonal skills.
- ○ **Example**: In **education**, teachers will still be essential for fostering creativity, empathy, and critical thinking among students. While AI can assist with personalized learning, the emotional intelligence and human connection that teachers provide cannot be replaced by machines.

4. **Leverage AI in Your Field**:
   - ○ Professionals should seek out tools and platforms powered by AI that can streamline their work and increase productivity. For example, those in **finance** can use AI-powered tools for risk assessment and fraud detection, while **marketing professionals** can utilize AI for targeted advertising and customer segmentation. By integrating AI into their daily workflows, professionals can stay ahead of industry trends and increase their efficiency.

o **Example**: A **financial analyst** can use AI tools to predict stock trends based on historical data, giving them an edge in making informed investment decisions. Similarly, a **graphic designer** can use AI to assist with tasks like creating layouts or selecting color schemes, allowing them to focus on more innovative aspects of design.

The Importance of Continuous Learning and Adaptability

As AI continues to evolve and shape industries, the most successful professionals will be those who embrace **continuous learning** and **adaptability**. To stay competitive in an AI-driven world, individuals must be committed to acquiring new skills and knowledge, as well as staying up to date with the latest developments in their industry. Professionals who are adaptable and proactive about learning will be better equipped to thrive as AI technologies continue to change the workplace.

1. **Lifelong Learning Mindset**:
   o The concept of **lifelong learning** is becoming more critical than ever. Professionals need to stay curious, continuously develop new skills, and embrace emerging technologies to remain relevant in their careers. Online courses, certifications, workshops, and industry

conferences are excellent ways to keep learning and stay competitive.

- o **Example**: An **IT professional** may need to learn new programming languages, **data analysis techniques**, or **AI frameworks** to stay current with the latest tech developments. Similarly, **teachers** may benefit from learning about AI-powered education tools to enhance their teaching methods and engage students more effectively.

2. **Upskilling and Reskilling**:
   - o As AI reshapes the workforce, some jobs will be transformed, while others may disappear. To stay employed and remain competitive, professionals will need to **upskill** (learn new skills within their current role) or **reskill** (learn new skills for a different role). By taking proactive steps to reskill or diversify their expertise, individuals can future-proof their careers and take advantage of new opportunities created by AI.
   - o **Example**: **Amazon** has invested heavily in **upskilling programs** for its workers, helping employees transition to roles that require more technical expertise, such as cloud computing or AI management. This initiative allows employees to shift from roles at risk of automation to ones that are more resilient to technological changes.

3. **Adaptability in the Face of Change**:

- o The rapid pace of AI development means that professionals must be adaptable to evolving technologies and industry trends. This requires a mindset that is open to change, willing to experiment with new tools, and flexible in the face of uncertainty. Being adaptable also means being able to pivot and take on new roles as the nature of work continues to shift.
- o **Example**: In the **customer service** industry, **chatbots** powered by AI are being used to handle routine inquiries, but customer service representatives who can manage more complex issues and offer human empathy will still be in high demand. Professionals who adapt to the evolving role of AI and focus on improving their interpersonal and problem-solving skills will continue to thrive.

4. **Developing Digital Literacy**:
   - o As AI becomes integrated into almost every field, it is crucial for professionals to be digitally literate. This means understanding the basics of AI and how it works, as well as the ethical implications of using AI systems. Professionals need to know how to interact with AI tools, how to use AI-generated data, and how to apply AI in their specific roles.
   - o **Example**: **HR professionals** may not need to become AI developers, but understanding how AI-powered

recruitment tools work and being able to effectively collaborate with tech teams is essential for making informed decisions about how AI should be used in hiring.

Real-World Example: Future-Proofing Your Career in AI Industries

AI industries are growing rapidly, and professionals in these fields must stay ahead of trends and developments to remain competitive. Careers in **data science**, **machine learning**, **robotics**, and **AI ethics** are flourishing as more organizations adopt AI technologies. Here are some practical steps for professionals looking to future-proof their careers in AI-driven industries.

1. **Investing in AI Education**:
   - For those interested in AI-related careers, investing in AI education is a key step in future-proofing your career. From specialized online courses to university degrees in AI and machine learning, education provides the foundation for working with cutting-edge technologies.
   - **Example**: Professionals interested in becoming **data scientists** or **machine learning engineers** can take online courses through platforms like **Coursera**, **edX**, or **Udacity**. Many universities also offer dedicated AI programs that teach essential skills like coding, data analysis, and deep learning.

2. **Networking in AI Communities**:
   - ○ Building a network of professionals in the AI field is crucial for career growth. Joining **AI communities**, attending conferences, and participating in online forums can help you stay connected to the latest trends and job opportunities. Networking also provides insight into industry standards, challenges, and best practices, which can be invaluable as you navigate your career.
   - ○ **Example**: **LinkedIn AI groups**, **Google AI meetups**, and conferences like **CES** or **NeurIPS** are excellent places to connect with industry leaders and peers, share knowledge, and learn about job openings in the AI sector.

3. **Building Practical Experience**:
   - ○ Gaining practical experience through **projects**, **internships**, or **freelance work** is vital for professionals seeking to work in AI industries. Building a portfolio of AI-driven projects can help demonstrate your skills to potential employers and increase your chances of landing a job in AI.
   - ○ **Example**: Aspiring **AI engineers** can work on projects such as developing a **chatbot**, building a recommendation engine, or contributing to open-source AI projects on platforms like **GitHub**. Real-world experience is a powerful way to

showcase your skills to potential employers.

Summary

In this chapter, we discussed how professionals can **prepare for the future** by adapting to an **AI-driven workforce**. The key to thriving in this evolving landscape lies in embracing AI as a tool, developing interdisciplinary skills, focusing on creativity and emotional intelligence, and engaging in **continuous learning** and **upskilling**. Professionals must stay adaptable, future-proof their careers by gaining knowledge in AI-related fields, and embrace digital literacy to effectively interact with AI systems.

We also highlighted **real-world examples** of future-proofing careers in AI industries, including **education**, **networking**, and gaining **practical experience**. By taking proactive steps to enhance their skills and stay connected to the AI community, professionals can successfully navigate the changing workforce and position themselves to thrive in an increasingly AI-driven world.